The
PATRIOT MISSION
Story

The PATRIOT MISSION Story
Reviews & Perspectives

"I am really stoked about *The PATRIOT MISSION Story*; it is a great, heartfelt book and a vitally important project for Patriotic Americans to tackle, RIGHT NOW! Personally, I will do whatever I can do to help The PATRIOT MISSION succeed in a big way.

The PATRIOT MISSION is such an incredible approach to what this dying nation needs right now to help solve the enormous problems we face as a free people, it gives us something meaningful to do to solve the seemingly insurmountable problems that America and Americans face today! It seems like everybody can and does write about the problems we face today, but only a few have come even close to spelling out the solutions like Steve does!

Rebuilding America is an enormous undertaking, but Steve has it so well thought out that it is easy to see. Steve has done a masterful job mapping out this huge problem and its simple piece by piece solution, that every American can play a part in saving this once, and soon to be, again, exceptional country of ours! God bless America, and God bless you, Steve Olds, for *The PATRIOT MISSION Story!*"

—**GERRICK BUSL**
Port St. Lucie, Florida

"I have read *The PATRIOT MISSION Story* and endorse it 130%. I have spent 20 years in a $400 million sales steel company, 19 years as an entrepreneur with 5 companies, and 11 years as a fighter pilot in the United States Military...the greatest military force in the world.

I was honored to be able to read this fantastic piece of Patriotism and support the concept to "Get the USA back to the people who believe in small business and the power of God."

—**DICK CANTNER, Lt. Colonel, USAR**
Vero Beach, Florida

★★★★

"If you love America and believe in the liberty and Freedoms that our Constitution provides for us, then you need to read *The PATRIOT MISSION Story*.

If you consider yourself a true patriot or if you feel a strong entrepreneurial spirit, then you need to read *The PATRIOT MISSION Story*.

I have known Steve Olds since 1997, and I know the love he has for our country. Out of that love he has developed a passion for saving and rebuilding America through the POWER of Small Business. In this book, Steve has mapped out strategies for "We the People" to ultimately choose one of two options:

1. **America Destroyed**
1. **America Rebuilt**

Considering the current path our country is on, each of us needs to choose."

—**JERRY CARLSEN, Voice & Data Cabling Contractor for 26 Years,**
Vero Beach, Florida

★★★★

"Steve Olds has done it again! Timely information, timely call to action, and finally the time has come to remember the dream of creating and living in a value driven country. Great job and I'm proud to support the vision, mission, and purpose of *The PATRIOT MISSION Story*."

—MARK EHRLICH, Business Coach;
Speaker and Author
California

★★★★

"*The PATRIOT MISSION Story* is a wake-up call every small business owner and entrepreneur should hear. It outlines how and why our country is on a slippery slope between big government and free enterprise. He points out that as Americans blindly accept more government and regulations, we are abdicating our responsibilities as citizens. In doing so, we're stifling the very entrepreneurial spirit on which this country was founded.

Fortunately this book isn't just another "the sky is falling" read that leaves you hanging for a solution. Steve Olds not only describes a solution, he also delivers it in detail. He presents a clear and practical blueprint for rebuilding America through small business.

Don't sit passively on the fence waiting for someone else to do the heavy lifting. Read the book, get engaged, and help make a difference that can last for generations."

—PHIL FARIS, Business Development Consultant; Coach;
Speaker and Author
Illinois
http://www.philfarisassociates.com

★★★★

"Steve Olds has done a great service to America by writing *The PATRIOT MISSION Story*. It inspires courage and action. There is hope for our country with the plan he has laid out. The application of his experiences as a fighter pilot to the threats America faces today is brilliant. There are serious problems facing the United States, but Steve Olds provides tremendous answers. Every American needs to read this book!"

—**WILLIAM J. FEDERER,** Author
St. Louis, Missouri
http://www.AmericanMinute.com

"In a time when busy people are consumed by their immediate surroundings, a man with a vision for America, as it was designed by our forefathers, emerges to bring us back to America's foundation.

Steve Olds is a relentless believer and a visionary, a man who cares so deeply about all of us and about our nation, that he would embark on a project of a magnitude so grand and so ambitious that it could be the pivotal turning point in America's direction toward triumphant victory and freedom, or the ultimate failure. What a privilege and responsibility we all have to stand along with Steve, and with God, to empower the next generations of this nation to turn the tide of hope toward free enterprise and a hope for a better future for all of us."

—**KELLY FISCHER,** Top Producing Realtor®, Broker Associate
Vero Beach, Florida
http://www.KellySoldMyHome.com

"Steve Olds and PATRIOT MISSION understand that free people affecting private business endeavors are the most prolific mechanism of human productivity known to mankind; and that the Genesis and core sustainability of America's unequaled economic strength in the world is her commitment to private property rights and her market driven, free enterprise system. The leaders at PATRIOT MISSION also understand that these dynamics are among the most powerful forces on Earth to promote and protect all aspects of human freedom. Their stated goal of "Rebuilding America through the Power of Small Business" is one that all Americans should fully embrace.

I had the privilege to meet with PATRIOT MISSION's management team for several hours to learn about their grassroots capitalism model: The MADE IN THE USA Project. The strategy Steve and Co-Founder Greg Land have designed is unique because it focuses at the county level and engages the community to promote entrepreneurship in a new generation. Their commitment to unleash the free enterprise spirit in every county, city, and parish in our Nation before 2020 is aggressive and timely. I support their efforts in Maricopa County, the State of Arizona and, ultimately, across America."

—**TRENT FRANKS, United States Congressman,**
Representing the 8th District of Arizona
http://www.TrentFranks.com

"*The PATRIOT MISSION Story* serves as an anthem to the next generation of voters and reminds everyone about the power of the entrepreneurial spirit. Never before has there been such a timely manuscript laying out a solid plan to restore America back to its greatness. This is a must read book."

—**CHARLES A. JENSEN**, President, Politics on the Rocks
Scottsdale, Arizona
http://www.politicsontherocks.com

"The PATRIOT MISSION. That just sounds good, doesn't it? Every patriot should have a mission, and in fact we all do. That mission is to declare, defend, and deploy the greatness of this nation we call the United States of America. United States. That's another good sound, isn't it? To be united in something that is good is such a privilege, an honor. Every man, woman, and child in this nation has that honor, that privilege. The question we must all answer is—what are we doing with it? Are we taking that responsibility in our hands and hearts and doing our part to perpetuate it? Or are we sitting idly by as those who wish to do us harm walk through our front door to have their way?

I've had the blessing of knowing and working alongside of Steve Olds for a couple of decades now, and there is no one more determined to fulfill the privilege of being a patriot than this man. He has put his life on the line in his military service. He has put his fortune on the line in the business sector. He has put his sacred honor on the line by taking a public stand against the tyranny in many sectors of our nation that seek to do us harm. That is the kind of patriot I'm honored and proud to call my friend.

Read *The PATRIOT MISSION Story* with an open mind and heart. Let it ask you the tough questions about where you stand and if you will just watch or wade into the fray. Be bold, like Steve and so many other small businessmen and women in the country who will not bow to bad times, bad governing, bad media, or bad ideas. This is your blueprint. The heavy lifting has been done. Let's pull together to put America back in her place as the most prosperous, giving, inspiring nation on the planet.

- I'm proud to be an American.
- I'm proud to know and call Steve Olds my friend.
- And I'm proud to stand with and work to fulfill the PATRIOT MISSION."

—DR. WILLIAM D. GREENMAN, President, Purpose International, USA
President, Purpose International Ministries, Kenya, Africa;
President, Lord & Demerest, Inc, Marketing Management Services
—a small business
Franklin, Tennessee
http://www.MasterKeysofLife.com

"I love these United States of America.

Since their inception, the USA has shown the rest of the world what allowing freedom to the individual can do for productivity, advancement, and goodwill in all areas of human endeavor.

Throughout the history of the USA there have always been a group of unsung heroes who exemplify the spirit of freedom that God blessed upon these United States—and those heroes are the entrepreneurs and small business owners who risk their time, money, and energy to build their businesses to be of service to others; dreaming of the day when they may harvest the fruits of their labor and know they have served their fellow citizens honorably, honestly, and profitably by providing goods, services, employment, and responsibly providing for their own families as well.

Quite frankly, this unique idea of the freedom of a self-governed individual has forever been a threat to those who want to be rulers rather than protectors of individual freedoms and responsibilities. And those self-serving "elites" work tirelessly to wear down the resolve of the free individual who gets up every day and makes a statement for personal freedom by continuously working to improve their life, their family's life, and the lives of those in their towns and cities all over the country and throughout the world.

When I first heard about The PATRIOT MISSION led by Steve Olds, I immediately let Steve know that I wanted to help in any way possible to get the word out, and be involved in helping We The People regain our individual God-given rights of life, liberty, and the pursuit of happiness that our great U.S. Constitution was designed to protect.

It is We The People who ultimately must protect and defend the U.S. Constitution from all enemies; this cannot be delegated. It must be done by each individual, their family, their community, and their state—upward from the grassroots and combining all who treasure individual freedoms into a nation-wide movement.

All across America people want leadership, real leadership. Leaders that will step up and shine the light on the pathway back to the true track of what has and will continue to make the USA the shining light of freedom in the world. Entrepreneurs and small business owners have the ability to do this. We can and must lead the way to reform our country back to its principled roots of freedom and justice for all.

I encourage you to read *The PATRIOT MISSION Story* to learn how we can take action together. Individual freedom is much too precious to lose; your children and your generations to come are depending on you and me.

A few years ago a friend of mine said something to me that I now paraphrase to you:

If you're going to take a stand later, you might as well take a stand now.

I hope you'll decide now to stand with me, Steve Olds, The PATRIOT MISSION, and all the other heroes I know and cherish as entrepreneurs and small business owners across this great land that God has blessed so much."

—**MARK HENDRICKS**
Trilby, Florida
http://www.TheMarkHendricks.com

"Steve Olds has put to paper what most have us have been feeling but have been unable to explain. Our country has forgotten its past, but more importantly, has stopped teaching the current generation about the major sacrifices made by our founders to create the only form of "Judeo-Christian" self-government in the history of mankind.

One of these founders, Patrick Henry, said it best: "It cannot be emphasized too strongly or too often that this great nation was founded, not by religionists, but by Christians, not on religions, but on the gospel of Jesus Christ!" Through the PATRIOT MISSION, Steve recaptures that same vision for America but more importantly has created a simple plan for every one of us to rebuild it person-by-person, family by family, business-by-business, in a ground-swell from the bottom up.

I am in total support of this plan and praying that other Americans, including those in government now, to be revived by this call to remember our source of life. 'Know that the Lord, He is God, it is He who has made us and it was not we ourselves'—Psalm 100:3"

—**RICH HENNESSEY,** Entrepreneur, New Ventures Advisor; and Christian
Vero Beach, Florida
http://www.RichHennessey.com

"*The PATRIOT MISSION Story*—defining today in America; looking to the future of America; a pleasant walk down the road of some memorable moments in American History; and a reminder about some folks who were willing to make a difference. Now to the question, what can each of us do that will make the future better for our children, our grandchildren, and the generations to come? Read this book.

I have known Steve and his family for 20 years. Steve and Nancy are proud to be Americans and have shared their patriotism with their family, friends, and community. The old saying 'The hand(s) that rocks the cradle rules the world' is verifiable. Steve's background has certainly led him to write *The PATRIOT MISSION Story*.

Read this book. Make decisions that will be honorable and that will make you proud of the person you see in the mirror."

—**FAYE HYATT,** Mother; Grandmother; Mentor
Lake Wales, Florida

"Steve Olds is a man who loves America. He is a true Patriot and entrepreneur. Over the past 10 years, I have had the great opportunity and privilege of associating and working with Steve on various business projects and know that he is a man good character and integrity. He has served valiantly in the military to help defend America.

In his book, *The PATRIOT MISSION Story*, Steve reveals a roadmap and strategy for rebuilding America by developing business, entrepreneurship, and leadership. This is more than a book. It is a mission to unite America and create true freedom. I hope you will take Steve's message to heart."

—**AL JOHNSON,** Customer Attraction Marketing Consultant
Mesquite, Texas
http://www.customerattractionmarketing.blogspot.com

"It is an honor and privilege to know Steve Olds, a fellow brother in Christ, and a true example of American grit, fortitude, and strength. This book further personifies his patriotism, love of county, and long lineage of the family faith from which he hails.

When I offered to review *The PATRIOT MISSION Story*, I was overwhelmed with the fine detail, the examples of true American heritage and perfect layman's terms describing the blueprint of recovery through entrepreneurial ownership and the foundation of PATRIOT MISSION.

When one is reminded of the many stories of our Founding Fathers of this great nation, a majority of whom preachers who gave of their entire life savings, only to die penniless for their noble and righteous cause, one must always remember their unwavering faith in the Providence of almighty God. It is a reminder of the fresh fire this great nation once again needs to take heed to continue to remain the greatest nation on Earth.

The quote a passage in *The PATRIOT MISSION Story*: "As for me and my family, we will serve the Lord and fight for Freedom in America."

May God corporately bless you Steve, your personal and PATRIOT MISSION family … and may God Bless the United States of America!!!"

—**KURT JORDAN**, SemperVigilo Group, Inc., Chief Investigator;
Fellow Patriot, Christian
Vero Beach, Florida
http://www.svgllc.org

★★★★

"All my life I admired America from afar. I first visited the USA in the early nineties, and loved it. It was not long after that, that I was able to convince my new bride that America was the place for us to seek out our place in the sunshine and do something new and 'out of the box'.

We immigrated (legally) over here in the mid 1990s in search of the American Dream (right in the middle of the Clinton-Lewinsky Saga).

After living in Africa all my life and travelling in Europe, I often wondered how this enormous country of over 300 million people could live at peace with each other under one central government. Amazing when you consider how relatively small but fragmented Europe is, or that South Africa (which is about the size of Texas), my birth country, prides itself on having 11 official national languages.

I quickly realized that there is something very special about America, the people, the system, the ideals and Constitution under which she was founded.

The idea that you can go out and start a business, or be anyone or anything you want while in search of your personal 'life, liberty and happiness' appealed to me and my love of small business and consulting to small business owners.

Over the years I have become increasingly concerned and disappointed that 'Real' Americans take what the founders set up, and what this great country offers everyone for granted, and moan and groan their way through life. An entitlement mentality and laziness was creeping in. This is becoming epidemic with the entitlement attitude and way of life being actively promoted by our current out of control government. As citizens we have dropped our guard and allowed government to grow and take over all facets of American life.

The 'Regulation Nation' is strangling small business everywhere, and unless you play ball in the 'crony capitalist' games, your chances of making it big in business are increasingly slim. Especially if the feds in the alphabet soup of big government agencies train their sights on you (IRS, DEP, OSHA, EPA).

America was founded by dreamers, thinkers, regular people, farmers, and small business people. Not one of them was a professional politician. Contrast that with today where America is 'ruled' by an 'elite' cadre of professional politicians, some of whom have never held a real job. They will do, or say anything, to stay in power while furthering their aims of total control.

Having grown up in Africa I have fought and seen firsthand the evils of socialism. How socialism has destroyed people and nations, and turned a wonderful continent which could have been the bread basket of the world into a 'basket case'.

Today I look out on an America that I do not recognize. This is not the America that I uprooted my family and moved 8500 miles across the world to create a better life for ourselves, our children, and others.

What I see now is an out of control big government, a nation intentionally divided across racial, gender, and economic lines.

A nation where the government picks winners and losers, and pits one group against another.

A nation where the government is intent on building the numbers of people reliant on government for everything, while stealing or redistributing the wealth of those still employed or in business to pay for these programs.

A nation on the decline—morally, spiritually, economically, and politically.

As Americans we need to wake up and act before it is too late. It is not hopeless but we need to act now.

I proudly stand with Steve Olds and other patriots like him to stop the tide and hopefully turn this once great country around. Steve has laid out a practical and very detailed game plan. 'Think Global—Act Local.'

By starting locally in our communities with local business and growing that movement nationally, we can impact, energize, and 'Rebuild America through the Power of Small Business'.

I am proud to say Steve is a patriot, my friend and business partner, who has 'put his life, his future, his fortune, and his sacred honor' on the line for America.

Read *The PATRIOT MISSION Story*, be encouraged, get involved, join the movement, and 'make a difference.'"

—**GREG LAND**, Marketing and Business Consultant;
Entrepreneur; Patriot; Christian family man
Vero Beach, Florida

"I've been searching for an outlet to answer an important personal question. How could I make a difference in America? I so long to help my beloved country find its way back to sanity. Now I've found it, it's in *The PATRIOT MISSION Story*! This book invited me into the great adventure of saving America and I'm all in.

Yes, I already have a life and a business to run, but where will I be without the America I grew up in. You owe it to yourself and your generations to find where you fit in and play your part in saving America. There's no time to waste, everyone is welcome, but we're not waiting for anyone. So saddle up and read this book tonight!"

—**ALAN E MEYERS**, CEO Michigan Marriage Tools
Cadillac, Michigan
http://www.LifeGivingMarriage.com

"Steve is a visionary for the times. Much like President Kennedy's charge to send man to the moon, or Martin Luther King, Jr.'s challenge for society to provide equal opportunity for all people, regardless of their color, through the PATRIOT MISSION, Steve is calling Americans to reverse our current direction by starting an Entrepreneurial Revolution that will create the spark that lights the candle to guide the steps of the current generation of Americans back to the path of success: spiritually, economically, and politically. The map has been drawn and the course set for America to re-establish itself as the greatest nation in the world. Now it's up to each one of us individually to take positive action that will make a difference."

—DREW MILES, CEO Pathfinder Business Strategies
Sebastian, Florida
http://www.PFBS.com

"When author Steve Olds took his Commissioning Oath as an officer and F-15 fighter pilot, he vowed to 'Support and defend the Constitution of the United States against all enemies, foreign or domestic…' With his combat missions over enemy airspace in Iraq complete, Olds trained his sights on the domestic front, exchanging missiles for a manuscript; a flight suit for a business suit.

In his inaugural book *The PATRIOT MISSION Story*, Olds continues his fight to protect American interests (this time from within), penning what may well become the catalyst, organizational playbook, and foundational steppingstone for galvanizing the efforts of millions of individuals, entrepreneurs, and small business owners—providing the creative spark for a national grassroots movement to rally around the beliefs and values that made this country great and worth fighting for.

In this impassioned and soaring treatise, Olds skillfully articulates two very different paths forward (and their dramatically different outcomes), before exhorting his readers to join him in recapturing nothing less than the historical sweep and national scale of America's legacy greatness. With a flair for the dramatic, the author deftly combines personal stories with political currency; seamlessly transitioning from strategic and visionary to practical and tactical and with a closing Call to Action and Call to Arms that will make you stand up and salute."

—**DOUGLAS O'BRYON**, CEO, Briarcliff Capital
Strongsville, Ohio
http://www.dougobryon.com

★★★★

"I first met Steve Olds in 1988 when he was assigned to the 27th Tactical Fighter Squadron as a young F-15 fighter pilot. Steve excelled in everything he did and refused to be second best in anything. Flying fighters requires commitment and passion—a commitment to excellence and a passion for defending the greatest nation in the world—the United States of America.

Steve carried that commitment and passion to the Gulf War where he and his squadron were one of the first to deploy to Saudi Arabia. America and the rest of the world watched in awe as the greatest display of airpower ever witnessed was demonstrated for all to see.

Steve has been talking to me for over five years about his concern for America and the need to rebuild this country using the same principles and ethics that our founding fathers envisioned. He realizes that the future of this country rests in the hands of small businesses and entrepreneurs—people willing to risk it all to secure the promises of liberty and free enterprise. He also realizes he can't do this alone—it requires the commitment and passion of every entrepreneur out there, which is why he formed the PATRIOT MISSION.

Read the story of the PATRIOT MISSION. It outlines the principles and strategies required to reclaim the greatness that was once ours. There are no magic wands—only dedication and hard work can guarantee our children and grandchildren a future as bright as the one America's Greatest Generation gave to us. Steve Olds is a member of America's NEXT Greatest Generation—he has risked it all for this nation in wartime and is now on a mission to preserve the America we all know is possible for future generations."

—ROY "BUBBA" PARKER, Colonel, United States Air Force (Retired)
Mansfield, Texas

"I am mightily impressed by the clear thinking and writing that you have put together to describe what your PATRIOT MISSION is and a "how to" series of steps taken to complete that mission by using the innate power of small businesses and their owners to rebuild our now failing economy and our way of life. I am equally impressed by your capacity to get to know and then collaborate with a person like Mr. Michael Gerber—and his famous success in the E-Myth evolution.

My confidence in you means a strong chance of making PATRIOT MISSION a success. For I have known you and your broad gauged family—directly—over a 30 year span of time. It began well before your mastery of supersonic aircraft in combat, to your dad, whose career in the FBI overlapped my own with the CIA, and our cooperation at street levels to bring down an alleged 'unbeatable enemy' like the Soviet Union.

My evidence that you will succeed is based upon a simple sentence that men and women of your character exemplify. A memorial U.S. Marine Corps coin that I try to live by suits you as well; the opposite side of the imprinted Globe and Laurel of the USMC has the inscription: 'Surrender is NOT an Option.' Good luck and Godspeed to you and your organization."

—**JOHN "JACK "PLATT, Raised as an Army Brat;**
US Marine Corps Recon Battalion Officer; CIA field operator;
Retired this year from a small business

★★★★

"As a dad who indicated Father's Occupation as Entrepreneur on his youngest daughter's Birth Certificate some 41+ years ago, I believe the concept of PATRIOT MISSION is a must for America's future. Steve's thought-provoking, poignant, and focused approach to rebuilding America is very motivational.

When I first started reading the manuscript, I kept saying to myself, "Yeah, that's right, but that's nothing new to me…I've lived it for 40+ years. Then I realized it was the lead-up, the challenge for those who have never been on their own, never started a business. Without the ideas put forth and the PATRIOT MISSION being effectuated, I truly believe this nation is doomed to overall government control. I hope it is not too late.

PATRIOT MISSION's challenge is not to let the noise of others opinions drown out your own inner voice!"

—**CHARLES VARS, President, Vars Associates, Inc. (38 yrs)**
Amherst, New Hampshire

"As a 30 year retired Air Force Colonel and a 20 year entrepreneur, Steve's book really hit home with me. I too feel that the American way of life has changed dramatically over the last decades and America needs a real awakening regarding our future. I have watched the industrial might of this great nation disappear overseas and the wage earner become unemployed with little to no hope of ever engaging in their chosen industry again. It is only through the power of small businesses that America can have a resurgence to once again become the nation it once was when I was growing up.

The concept of the entrepreneur starting and growing a small business has always led the way to a better economy. How many people like Steve Jobs, Michael Dell, and Bill Gates are on the verge of creating a business but need assistance in today's regulation crazy government? It is our job to help them navigate the bureaucracy and provide the encouragement they need to succeed. Steve has created the method and it remains for us to execute the plan. Great job and I look forward to working with you!"

—**MARTIN J ZICKERT**, Colonel, United States Air Force (Retired);
America's Real Life Planners, LLC;
President, Veterans Council of Indian River County, Florida;
President, Vietnam Veterans of America Chapter 1038

The
PATRIOT MISSION
Story

The
PATRIOT MISSION
Story

A **BOLD** Blueprint to Rebuild America
through the Power of Small Business™

STEVE OLDS

Patriot Mission Press
Vero Beach, FL

© 2013 PATRIOT MISSION PRESS

All Rights Reserved.

No part of this publication may be reproduced or transmitted in any form or by any means, mechanical or electronic, including photocopying and recording, or by any informational storage or retrieval system, without permission in writing from the author or publisher (except by a reviewer, who may quote brief passages and / or show brief video clips in a review).

The following are Trademarks of PATRIOT MISSION and may not be used without permission.

- PATRIOT MISSION™
- The PATRIOT MISSION Story™
- Rebuild America through the Power of Small Business™
- PATRIOT MISSION PRESS™
- The POWER of Small Business™
- Celebrate Small Business™
- The MADE IN THE USA Project™
- Private Business Incubator™
- Backbone of America™
- Rebuild America System™
- Rebuild America Series™
- Patriot Speakers™

Disclaimer: The Publisher and the Author make no representation or warranties with respect to the accuracy or completeness of the contents of this work and specifically disclaim all warranties, including without limitation, warranties of fitness for a particular purpose.

Published by: PATRIOT MISSION PRESS
ISBN: 978-0-9898411-0-8 (Hardcover)
ISBN: 978-0-9898411-1-5 (Paperback)
ISBN: 978-0-9898411-2-2 (E-Book)
ISBN: 978-0-9898411-3-9 (Audio Book)

For more information contact:
PATRIOT MISSION PRESS
5976 20th Street, Suite 127
Vero Beach, Florida 32966
http://www.PatriotMissionPress.com, 855.867.3284

For information about PATRIOT MISSION Speakers
http://www.PatriotSpeakers.com
855.867.3284

Printed in the United States of America
Cover Design by Christine | christinetabor.com
Images by Thinkstock and iStock
Book Design by Dotti Albertine

Get your FREE Personal Blueprint to Rebuild America through the Power of Small Business™

Call Toll Free: 855.TO.REBUILD
(855.867.3284) or Visit
http://www.PatriotProfile.com

Receive a Bonus Subscription to the "Rebuild America Series™" when you claim your personal blueprint!

CLIENT: *Your Name*
PROJECT: *Rebuild America*

To Nancy

My Love. My Life.

CONTENTS

Acknowledgments   *xxv*
Foreword by Michael E. Gerber   *xxix*
Introduction   *xxxiii*

PART I
WHY REBUILD AMERICA?

Chapter 1	The Fading American Dream	3
Chapter 2	Blueprint of an American Entrepreneurial Revolution	7
Chapter 3	The Birth of The PATRIOT MISSION Story	15
Chapter 4	Combat Flashback	23
Chapter 5	7 Founding <u>LIBERTY</u> Principles	29
Chapter 6	"The Shining City on a Hill"	43

PART II
HOW CAN WE REBUILD AMERICA?

Chapter 7	BUILD Bold Leadership Teams in Every County, City, and Parish	63
Chapter 8	Mentorship – A Turning Point Toward the Future	71

Chapter 9	Massive Leadership Impact... in One Year!	75
Chapter 10	Developing Strong Local Leaders	85
Chapter 11	Growing Critical Assets in 3 Steps	91
Chapter 12	Step 1A: GROW Our Personal Capital	95
Chapter 13	Step 1B: GROW Our Professional Capital	103
Chapter 14	Step 2: GROW Our Political Influence	121
Chapter 15	Step 3: GROW Our Liberty	129

PART III
WHAT IS THE ACTION PLAN TO REBUILD AMERICA?

Chapter 16	Planning the Mission	137
Chapter 17	Rebuild America System™	145
Chapter 18	Stakeholders and Execution Plan	155
Chapter 19	Strategy #1 – Inspire a Nation	163
Chapter 20	The Impact of America's New Founders	173
Chapter 21	Strategy #2 – Implement Grassroots Chapters	183
Chapter 22	Grassroots Capitalism. County-by-County.	191
Chapter 23	Strategy #3 – Influence Global Entrepreneurship	203

PART IV
HOW CAN I WIN BY HELPING REBUILD AMERICA?

Chapter 24	The 2020 Storyline & Beyond	211
Chapter 25	"Fight's On"	217
References		*225*

ACKNOWLEDGMENTS

Over the last several years, I've had the opportunity to reflect on the incredible odyssey my entrepreneurial experience has taken over two decades. Candidly, I could write an entire book on how different people have helped me along the way.

For the moment, I'll simply share a couple of lines about a team of people who have played a direct role in my life, in many different ways, which helped me develop PATRIOT MISSION and this story. I apologize in advance to anyone I neglect to mention and humbly request your forgiveness. The acknowledgments are listed generally in the order of appearance in my life's storyline.

—**God**: I still find it hard to fathom the creator of the universe can love me for who I am when I do not deserve it. Thank you for loving me, saving me through your son Jesus' blood and giving me this inspirational vision to reclaim this wonderful land of America for you and your kids.

—**Mom & Dad**: My original cheerleaders, mentors, and unending supporters. Thanks, Mom, for the cheers and shooting stars from heaven since you went home to be with the Lord in 1989. Dad, your leadership, love, and friendship have sustained me. It's time for an executive meeting.

—**Cathy, Jenny & Betsy**: The three best little sisters a guy could ask for. You've always encouraged me, challenged me, and stood by me, even when I didn't deserve it.

—**Nancy, Savannah & Sarah**: I thought flying in combat was the most challenging career I could imagine. I've come to appreciate that being married to, or the child of, an entrepreneur is exponentially more difficult. Thank you for putting up with my dreams and standing with me. I love you more than words can express.

—**Sybil**: Mothers-in-law get a bad rap. You were amazing. I know you are dancing with Jesus!

—**Toni**: Thanks for loving my dad, playing a key role in our family, and always encouraging me.

—**Billy, Curt & Jason**: In different ways, as you three brothers have joined the family, you supported me in ways you will never know. Strength, courage, and commitment.

—**Don**: From ERHS to Det 330 to an awesome godfather, supporter, and friend. Thank you.

—**Dan**: Started at Princeton Ave, Friendly's with Doc, Santa Rosa and Dallas with MEG, and on to Annapolis with Cygnus. Steadfast and True.

—**Dr. Point**: From a wingman at MHG, CCI, Sloot's & Sam's gigs and on to the big time. I'm proud of you. Thanks for the wisdom on the PM Board.

—**Doc**: My brother, I know you are watching on the big screen, but your coaching never stops.

—**Bubba**: You taught a young pup how real leaders operate, especially when I didn't want to hear it.

—**Stick**: When there was no evidence to believe, you did. You never quit on me or my family.

—**Bishop**: You taught me about the death of a seed; and in my case more than one. Praise God.

—**Ms. Faye**: From the farm to math to family counseling to accounting to friendship at its finest.

—**Bartman**: You give new meaning to stalwart support. Thanks for the media coaching & PR.

—**Michael**: To my Dutch uncle who taught me it's still cool to be a dreamer.

—**Jeffro:** We've been practicing for a decade. Time to put Doc's stuff to work and train up the team. Don't pay us any mind... said the spider to the fly.

—**Sallie**: Your expertise, creativity and patience have been incredibly important to our ability to launch this mission.

—**Bryan**: In the darkest of days, you shared the hard Word and the blessings of the Kingdom.

—**Greg**: To my PATRIOT MISSION co-founder. Thanks for your friendship, insight, keen counsel and tireless effort to bring this story to fruition. The world is counting on us!

—**Drew**: You encouraged me to write this book and not take my eyes off PATRIOT MISSION.

—**Jerry**: Working the prototype in the trenches with me was a HUGE part of this book. Thanks for always being willing to help.

—**Jim:** Since CBMC days, you have been a friend, mentor, and counselor in many ways. Your Godly wisdom has been crucial.

—**DC**: Thanks for no excuses training and giving me hope for the next generation; in more ways than one.

—**Tripp**: It's good to have another strong guy on the team. Study hard. The pace is fast.

—**Duke**: Truly man's best friend. Thanks for getting me up at 4 a.m. to write this story.

FOREWORD

There's something about writing a book, just as there's something about reading one. The writing of course takes a level of courage, commitment, passion, and perseverance from the author more intimidating than the reader can possibly imagine. In this book, the story it tells of The PATRIOT MISSION was founded some years ago in the imagination and inspiration of my friend, fellow author, and fellow Patriot, Steve Olds.

A former jet pilot, a truly zealous patriot, and a lanky, tall guy who said to me one day during one of his 12 Dreaming Room experiences with me, "I've got it, Mr. Gerber, I've got it!" What he meant when he said that to me, was that he finally had come face to face with the Mission he is here on Earth to manifest. Which he now calls The PATRIOT MISSION. Which is the subject of this book, and which lives in the heart of Steve Olds. I told Steve then, that when he finally saw his book through—if he ever did—that I would be honored to write the Foreword to it.

Which is the purpose of my message to you, dear reader. Both to keep my promise to Steve Olds, as well as to share with you the other reason why I'm writing to you, the other reason I'm speaking to you now through the words on the page in front of you. The other reason is simple and straightforward: our country, America, is in trouble. (If you live in any country other than America, know that America was founded for all of us, not just for those who live in it right now. Which is why I think of it as "our country.")

Yes, as I write this epistle to you, it's August 1, 2013, and America is in trouble. And because America is in trouble, so are we all. And that's because America was founded upon a principle called freedom. At its heart, America is a testament to the word and the act of freedom. And so, if America is in trouble, so is freedom. And if freedom is in trouble, then so are we all.

So, why is America in trouble? Because we have become disconnected from our roots here. What I like to think of as our Founders' Roots. Our American Founders were men who saw in their minds' eye a future unlike any other. A future in which men were to be provided with a place to inhabit, built by them, just for them, built upon principles of freedom unlike any other principles. Freedom to think what one wishes to think. Freedom to act however one wishes to act. Freedom to believe in what one wishes to believe. Freedom to live however each and every one of us wishes to live. Freedom to congregate. Freedom to live by the laws created by free men.

Yes, I know you have all heard this before. But understand, please, that if America is in trouble—and she is—then while you've heard these words before, you've forgotten the meaning of them. And if you've forgotten the meaning of them, you might as well not have heard them at all. Which is what this book is about. This book is about America. This book is about freedom. This book is about the expression of freedom by ordinary people in everything they think, feel, live, and do.

This book is about a philosophy which says that the world was created by God, for man to live in the image of God, to express ourselves wholeheartedly, with the very same passion and conviction and integrity as our American Founders did. This book is about you. It is about what you do every day. It is about living the fullest life imaginable. It is about creating a world around you which is a testament to God's Greatness. It is also about working on your life, rather than simply working in it.

It's about the Great Law of Invention. The Law at the heart of Commerce. The Law which says that each and every one of us has been blessed with the opportunity to invent a life which is here to serve, to serve every one of us, to serve our lives, and to serve our future. To serve God's Creation. Which takes me back to the subject at hand: America is in trouble.

If America is, at its heart, a testament to Freedom, then it is as well a testament to the Great Law of Invention which is the Great Spring from which Free Commerce flows. Which is how and why America became in its short lived 200-plus years, the most economically vibrant country the world has ever known. Which is the root of our being. Which flows from the root which springs forward from God. Which lives within the idea of America: that we are founded in God's image. Which means we were born to create.

Which means that the product of America, when it is living in its full-blown spirit, is the vitality of growth. Which is the heart of Commerce. Which is the handmaiden of The Great Law of Invention. Which is what man is here to do. Which is what this book is about.

Which is what moved Steve Olds to come up to me that day in The Dreaming Room to say, "Mr. Gerber I've got it!" Which is why he wrote this grand book. Which is why Steve Olds is a patriot. Which is why you must read, and read, and read *The PATRIOT MISSION Story*!

With love, as Always,
Michael E. Gerber
Co-Founder, Chairman
Michael E. Gerber Companies™
Creator of The E-Myth Evolution™
P.O. Box 131195
Carlsbad, CA 92013
http://www.michaelegerber.com

INTRODUCTION

It was a hot, muggy summer morning in Maryland just outside the Washington Beltway. A lot of grown-ups complained about the heat, but I thought weather conditions were perfect to launch a new business. This would be my first foray into the brave new world of entrepreneurship.

I still remember how fired up I was. I pulled out planks of plywood from my dad's woodpile in the backyard and carefully placed them on top of assembled wooden crates and the milk box. Once the display table was verified to be sturdy on the corner of the driveway, I placed a folded, white bed sheet from the linen closet on top of the makeshift merchandise counter (I was sure Mom wouldn't mind).

Before preparing the samples, I wrote a brilliant advertising pitch using the blackest Magic Marker on the smoothest cardboard box I could find in the basement.

ICE COLD LEMONADE
Only 25¢ a Cup!
5 Cups for $1
Free Samples

Little did I know in the summer of 1973, I was actually launching a lifetime journey. At the time, all I really wanted was to make enough money to go to the movies or buy a toasted almond when the ice cream truck rolled through the neighborhood before dinner.

In my only food service industry endeavor, I learned many lessons including how much raw materials, ice, samples, cups, and spillage cost as well as the importance of a store's location. I appreciated the handful of customers who felt sorry for me, including my mom, a few neighbors, and the construction workers who happened to drive by around lunchtime. I discovered sitting at a lemonade stand waiting for people to show up was not as glamorous as I thought it would be.

I still smile when I think about my single day, entrepreneurial venture and the fact my parents encouraged me to give it a shot. Could they have explained to an eight-year-old boy all the reasons why this would likely be a failed venture? Sure, but I would probably not be writing about it 40 years later. I learned valuable, lifelong lessons that day and I got to be a kid.

Fast forward four decades and we hear stories of kids having their lemonades stand shut down and threatened with five hundred dollar fines for not having required permits. Bureaucrats happily explain about food safety, road hazards, sales tax, and fairness in restaurant advertising. Sad!

These two contrasting stories illustrate the crazy world we live in today. Entrepreneurs face massive regulatory and compliance burdens that crush creativity. America's economy is in a shambles and a frightening number of our fellow citizens believe government is the solution.

America is at a crossroads. Unlike other pivotal times in our history when Americans stood shoulder-to-shoulder and faced BIG challenges together, today we are a divided people. Unfortunately, many influential people prefer to fuel the chaos and widen the lines of division.

My purpose here is not to drill down into all the historical and geopolitical reasons why these divisions exist. Rather, I will focus on key principles and executable strategies which are foundational for America's survival, long term recovery and future success. We must reignite a financially vibrant economy and effectively reestablish strong leadership at home and abroad.

Throughout our time together, I will propose a detailed strategy to effectively reduce the division and begin to heal the country through a series of basic actions that serve our families, our businesses, and our communities. If we decide the USA is worth salvaging, I submit we can rapidly come together and solve our own problems which, in turn, will influence positive action by local, state, and federal politicians. Every American citizen and legal resident can have an impact, regardless of their experience in the entrepreneurial or small business worlds.

Why should you listen to me?

Fair question. I am an entrepreneur who is facing many of the same challenges you are. I am bound and determined to work with you and others who are committed to focusing on **BOLD** solutions. Rather than trying to impress you with my résumé, accomplishments, and stunning endorsements, I'd rather just share my personal story as we go through this discussion. You can decide if the ideas and strategy I offer, coupled with my experience and results, are credible.

I ask you to soak in *The PATRIOT MISSION Story* and let it encourage you. Take the time to rediscover your own story. Enjoy the flashbacks as you remember how you felt about America as a kid. Then consider the potential impact you can have on your own future should you decide to step up and help us Rebuild America right now. Finally, even if you don't yet have a family of your own, consider the impact on several generations of your kids and grandkids.

This is not a gloom and doom story; quite the contrary. This is a story of optimism.

There is hope, but we don't have a lot of time to get busy. I believe if we work together expeditiously, we can rescue America from the peril which she now faces.

When you have finished *The PATRIOT MISSION Story*, I want you to be inspired, encouraged, and motivated. Together, we can save our freedom and protect our liberty.

May God Bless the United States of America!

> Cheers,
> Steve Olds
> 2013

PART I

WHY REBUILD AMERICA?

> *"A house divided against itself cannot stand."*
>
> — Abraham Lincoln —

Chapter 1

The Fading American Dream

Every day in America, there are gazillions of books, articles, blog posts, television and radio programs produced to offer perspective on the geopolitical and economic reasons for the stiff headwinds we face. There are certainly plenty of politicians to hammer on both sides of the aisle, but then of course, we elected them. On top of these concerns, since 9/11/01 we have had to contend with radical Islamic terrorists who hate America and will kill us just because of who we are and what we believe.

So all in all, it's a pretty easy time to pursue the American Dream (sarcasm).

Over the past several years, I've interviewed countless entrepreneurs, small business owners, professionals, concerned citizens and young people who are incredibly frustrated. Regardless of political affiliation, there is a universal observation that government is making it harder and more expensive to do business and get work. Combined with years of little or no economic growth, it is a stressful time to be a shopkeeper or job seeker on Main Street, USA.

When you look at the numbers, according to the U.S. Small Business Administration, there are nearly 30 million small business owners in America, 73% of which are sole proprietors. This means in the aggregate, we are one of the largest constituency groups in the country, yet by our very nature as rugged individualists, we find ourselves very much alone.

Certainly there are local trade organizations and national groups claiming to represent the small business community. However, if you simply look at the trends and results, the key strategic indicators do not instill confidence. Whether you are an attorney from New York, a Florida citrus grower, a Midwest manufacturer or California software designer, the cost of doing business is off the charts, hiring is down, and the regulatory compliance burden is skyrocketing.

Entrepreneurs and small business owners are not the only frustrated people.

Citizens who live in local communities and want to support small businesses are watching strip malls, stand-alone stores, and decades old professional firms continue to disappear. When entrepreneurs shutter their companies, it means jobs are lost, goods and services are no longer available, and local economic growth slows or grinds to a halt.

Those who manage to keep their doors open generally must work harder with less people. Even in the best of times, there is always a turnover in business due to best practices, financial planning, market timing, etc., but in America at this moment in time, we are dealing with an epidemic of disastrous proportions.

The cost of education has gone through the roof and student loans are at an all-time high. College and high school graduates are looking for jobs in record numbers. In addition to this younger demographic, there are tens of millions of Americans who are underemployed or who have given up looking for work altogether. This is unacceptable.

On the other side of the equation, there are some small businesses that are doing well. They have prepared, built impressive intellectual property in their niche, created strong earnings, and saved a solid bankroll. In many cases they are able to capitalize on opportunities and are expanding. We can learn a lot from these entrepreneurial leaders.

At our core, we are 30 million problem solvers who want our businesses, families, and country to run well. As business people, our nature is to create solutions, but it is hard to wrap our arms around the enormity of these economic and political challenges. So most business owners strap on their flak jackets, keep their heads down, focus on the task at hand, and work very hard.

My observation since the economy began to tank in 2008 is many business people feel very stressed out, isolated, and alone. This includes employees, managers, owners, and to a large extent their families. Across the board, they are tired, worn out, and generally fed up because the media has largely promoted the expectation this is the 'new normal.'

As a party of one, I will admit my FED-UP METER IS PEGGED, but I beg to differ about the permanency of the situation. I believe we can change it and revitalize a spirit of optimism, hope, and success. People often ask: "What can I do about it?" This is where we have a choice.

Albert Einstein's definition of insanity comes to mind.

"Doing the same thing over and over again and expecting different results."

Those who believe we can change our circumstances ask a different question. "How can I help change it?" I contend this chaos creates a **massive opportunity** for entrepreneurs, small business owners, employees, concerned citizens, job seekers, and young people looking for a career.

What exactly is this massive opportunity?

We have the opportunity **To Rebuild America through the Power of Small Business**™!

Chapter 2

Blueprint of an American Entrepreneurial Revolution

Why Rebuild America? How can we possibly accomplish such an enormous task?

In this material, I will answer these questions in detail. Believe it or not, the solution is actually quite simple. The first step is to make the decision to take action. Currently in America we are still allowed to think for ourselves and make decisions. You have probably surmised, many of us have already made the decision to pursue the PATRIOT MISSION, which is in fact **To Rebuild America through the Power of Small Business**™.

If you decide the blueprint has merit, I will show you how you can become part of the solution without having to fall on your sword, write big checks to political organizations or march on Washington. You will discover as we rebuild the nation, each of our companies, communities, and citizens will get stronger and more successful. We will expand our networks, our revenue sources, and most importantly the impact on the next several generations. We will bring back citizen politicians who want to serve us and defend our liberty.

Here are a few things you will not find in our plan:

- There will be no new technological widgets that solve all our problems in 1.2 nanoseconds.

- There is no super-secret government sauce that will miraculously heal the economy and suddenly recapture our wasted time and tax dollars.
- You will not find a 73-page application for free government bailout cash with zero interest and a 100 year repayment / forgiveness / write-off schedule.

Here's what you will discover:
- A sound model that works every time it is tried (it has been used successfully since our country was founded).
- A plan built on core American principles that serve as a bedrock regardless of political affiliation, religious point of view, or personal heritage.
- A group of like-minded people who are as passionate about saving America as you are.
- A simple way to use and share this plan with others (hint… we each have a unique story).
- A practical, hands-on opportunity to help save America before she self-destructs.

Let's get started.

DEFINITION: **Revolution—noun**—a far-reaching and drastic change, especially in ideas, methods, etc[1].

There is no doubt we are facing tough times. This is nothing new for Americans. As an entrepreneur, small business owner, husband, dad, frustrated citizen, former military officer, and student of history, I believe there is a lot we can learn from those who have gone before us.

In 1776, fifty-six businessmen and leaders stood shoulder-to-shoulder and risked everything when they signed their names to this powerful statement… "And for the support of this Declaration, with a firm reliance on the protection of Divine Providence, we mutually pledge to each other our Lives, our Fortunes, and our sacred Honor."

They were very frustrated with the British government which was dictating, controlling, and taxing nearly every element of their lives (*sounds vaguely familiar*). These men shared a common set of principles for which they were willing to risk everything they held dear.

Think about that for a minute.

When is the last time you got together for a strategic planning session and mapped out a grandiose, world-changing plan that ended with you signing your own death warrant? Each of the 56 colonists knew they would hang if their ragtag militia failed to defeat the British Crown, which enjoyed the most powerful military in the world at the time.

I submit the challenges we face today in the United States of America are at least as big if not bigger than the one our Founders faced. You can relax. I'm not going to ask you to sign a blood oath or put your name on a document that will be circulated to government agencies. I'm simply making the point that if we do not recognize the peril we face and take substantive action to correct the path we are on, then we will have lost the fight.

Fortunately, many of us have family members or are old enough ourselves to remember some of the most amazing American success stories like winning World War II and the Apollo mission to the moon. There are countless technological miracles like the Internet, cellular phones, and modern medicine that have all largely been born of American ingenuity and financial prowess.

One of the great tragedies in America today is there are so many people living here who have no idea why our country was founded or how the framers took enormous care to protect our liberty. They never studied what our forefathers went through to create our magnificent country. Millions of Americans do not understand our Founders' faith and why they relied on "Divine Providence" to guide them to write the Declaration of Independence and win the Revolutionary War.

Huge numbers of our citizens and government officials forsake and dismiss the U.S. Constitution as an old, outdated set of rules rather than the magnificent, inspired, unique work that it is. Of course, when accurate history is systematically removed from our education system, what else would you expect? Let's not go down that track for now; that could be an entire book of its own.

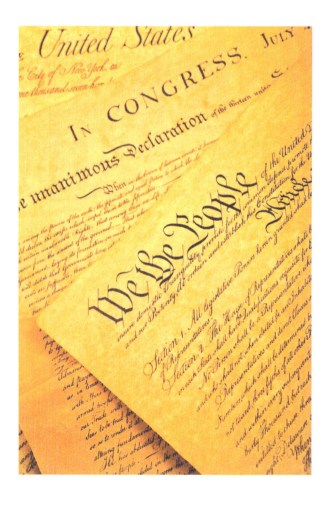

What is an Entrepreneurial Revolution?

In the same way the Founders led a revolution, we must wrest America's defeat from our enemies, which now primarily lie within our borders. The enemies of ignorance, apathy, financial stupidity, political correctness, and worst of all, hopelessness. We have the opportunity to apply our entrepreneurial skills, passions, dreams, and sweat to lead an effort to make sure our Founders and the generations since who have given their all to protect our country did not die in vain.

You may think this is a bit melodramatic, but please hear me out.

As I'll share with you in more detail shortly, I am a combat veteran. I know what it is like to raise my right hand and promise to protect and defend the Constitution of the United States of America against all enemies foreign and domestic. Although I left active military service, the oath I swore never left me. I have experienced the adrenaline rush of combat with hostile forces intent on killing me so I would never make it home to see my bride and newborn baby girl. I have watched my fellow comrades in arms make the ultimate sacrifice.

The good news is we are Americans. We understand freedom in a way that no other people on the face of the Earth do. We have freed more people, saved more lives, given more of our own blood and treasure than any people in history. The bad news is we have become complacent.

We have allowed our nation to forget its history and become mired in a self-serving entitlement mentality, punctuated with authoritarian greed. That will not change unless there is a massive movement to speak truth and drive effective action into the very grassroots of our country.

PATRIOT MISSION is speaking that truth and driving action; county-by-county.

We need to go far beyond talking. We must demonstrate what it looks like to live out our core principles. We must lead by example and be worthy of following. We must inspire a new generation with ideas and practices that produce results and leave America in much better shape than she is right now. We are equipped to do it and God willing, we will complete the mission.

Some citizens will suggest America's global influence, power, and position are not as important or appropriate as they were in years past. They believe international governance should be run by committee. That would be fine except for one thing. Look at the track record of the other major players in the global community.

What other countries have freed millions of people from dictatorships, despotism, and terror? China is still a Communist country. Russia is reverting back to its Soviet and KGB roots, and Europe's socialist economy is dying. Who do third world countries call when there is a disaster? America is a generous and giving country.

As long as our Constitution remains the centerpiece of our nation, it is "WE THE PEOPLE" who decide our future, not the government. We believe America's Problems will be solved by a core group within the entrepreneurial community who decides to take massive action and then follows through. Our strategy has been very carefully designed to leverage small, incremental changes made by individuals across the national landscape to create a cumulative and massive impact.

PATRIOT MISSION's long-term strategy is to influence multiple generations of Americans, including those who will be born in the coming years and decades. The short-term plan is to implement local grassroots chapters in each of America's 3141 counties, independent cities, and parishes before 2020. Our work is truly unifying because it focuses on the practical realities of small business, entrepreneurship, and jobs as opposed to bloviating political speech.

The entrepreneurial revolution blueprint is founded on seven **LIBERTY** principles and will be accomplished by executing the PATRIOT MISSION Dream, Vision, Purpose, and Mission.

7 Founding LIBERTY Principles

1. **We believe** the economic Backbone of America™ is powered by the **LEADERSHIP** of Small Business Founders, employees, and their families.

2. **We believe** providentially inspired American **INGENUITY** has created the strongest economy and most generous society the world has ever known.

3. **We believe** it is important to elect leaders who share a common **BELIEF** in our Judeo-Christian heritage and the magnificence of the U.S. Constitution.

4. **We believe** **ENTREPRENEURSHIP** is the primary economic means to inspire men and women to pursue their dreams and achieve prosperity.

5. **We believe** Life, Liberty, and the Pursuit of Happiness are put at tremendous **RISK** by those who reject capitalism and promote excessive public spending.

6. **We believe** Personal Property Rights and the Free Enterprise System are **TIMELESS** constitutional cornerstones upon which America was founded.

7. **We believe** it is crucial to inspire **YOUNG** citizens to become tough-minded, ethical entrepreneurs so they can help create long-term solutions for America.

Our Dream is to **LEAD** Americans to Rediscover "The Shining City on a hill."

Our Vision is to **BUILD** a Bold Leadership Team in every county, city, and parish.

Our Purpose is to **GROW** our Capital, Political Influence, and Liberty.

Our Mission is **To Rebuild America through the Power of Small Business**™.

In the upcoming chapters, I will bring each of these statements to life with practical applications, historical context, and personal experiences so you can get a feel for how seamlessly these pieces fit together. These ideas are not new. This works because of the unique manner we have put them together. Based on years of research, interviews, and personal experience, we believe millions of people carry these passions in their hearts and minds.

The PATRIOT MISSION Story is your story and my story. It is the story of those who will lead by example and get in the trenches to rebuild America on solid ground. Until now, people have had to wonder where they could turn to find the camaraderie of fellow Americans who would stand with them. You found us. Welcome home.

Chapter 3

The Birth of The PATRIOT MISSION Story

Before a story can be written, you first have to develop a storyline. Typically the storyline lays out the plot for a production with all the characters including the villains, heroes, and bystanders. A good storyline will integrate a powerful theme to connect the audience with a much deeper meaning beyond the tangible elements of the drama. One of the hallmarks of a powerful storyline is when you can see yourself in the story and feel the emotion as the action unfolds.

The best part about creating a storyline is the writer gets to decide how it turns out. The American storyline has been chock full of action ever since Christopher Columbus and his brave explorers set sail in 1492. More than half a millennium of history gives us great material to tell the rest of the story (as Paul Harvey would say). As we do our research, we have access to the wisdom of the ages in her archives, provided we are willing to dig in and dust off the pages of history. Right now America has plenty of good guys and bad guys. She has lots of drama going on. Now it's time to decide how the story ends… or at least continues to the next few generations.

Here's a complicating factor.

There is more than one group of writers who are competing to tell the winning narrative. We do not have the luxury of time to sit back and relax while we pontificate about utopia. As a matter of fact, some would argue the false attraction of a utopian state run by those who "know best" has created many of the most significant challenges we face.

We are on a deadline to finish the storyline, pitch it to the investors, recruit the actors, jump in the trenches, produce the scenes, get feedback from a screening audience, make edits, create the marketing strategy, promote the message to the masses, launch it nationwide, captivate a new generation of Americans, inspire them to rebuild the country, and reestablish U.S. leadership of the free world. Other than that, this should be a standard entrepreneurial adventure (more sarcasm).

America's story is about "WE THE PEOPLE," which is not just a catchy phrase; it is the foundation of our government and the most amazing experiment in human history. It is the idea that free people can and should decide what is best for them, not autocratic rulers. Whether our families are descendants of the Pilgrims or if we are first generation naturalized citizens, as Americans, we share a common and unique bond. I believe this story is ingrained in the hearts of men and women across America, but for the most part it has been in cold storage. Our job is to warm up the American people in an exciting, hopeful, productive, and experiential way.

The PATRIOT MISSION Story is America's story told through the eyes of her people.

I've come to realize that every time period in our lives, even the painful ones, can make a positive contribution to our personal story. Our individual stories in turn merge with other people's stories to create a life tapestry of sorts.

Have you ever seen one of those quilts that are made up of individually designed squares?

America is like the quilt. Each of us and the story we choose to live is one of the "squares" sewn into the fabric of our nation. In order to put the story in context, I'd like to share a little bit about my background and a few relevant experiences so you understand how my "square" influenced the design of the PATRIOT MISSION plot.

I grew up in Clinton, Maryland, about eight miles outside of Washington, D.C. Our family of six lived near the back gate of Andrews Air Force Base (AFB), where I regularly watched the military jets come and go. My dad was a naval officer and a career FBI Special Agent. Mom chose to stay home and raise my three sisters and me along with our little dog Twinkles. I know… what kind of a name is that? We guessed Twinkles was a cocker spaniel and poodle mix. In December 1976, Mom found her starving to death at a Christmas tree lot and brought her home with the tree for one night that turned into more than a decade. But I digress.

I had a number of formative experiences as a kid that impacted my eventual foray into entrepreneurship. Raising a family of six in the D.C. Metro market on a government salary wasn't an easy chore. In the 1970s, a lot of moms went to work to supplement the family income and re-launch a career they may have started before kids. My folks made a choice to have Mom stay home and continue our education after school. Of course, I didn't realize we were continuing our schooling; I thought Mom was just serving as a taxi driver to my soccer and T-ball games in between my sisters' dance lessons.

As a young kid I began to learn about small business from my parents.

At the time I wasn't all that mesmerized with Mom and Dad's great entrepreneurial skills; it was just another chore on my list before I could go out and play. They started a home-based business selling candles. My mom loved designing unique wax creations. She embedded Chesapeake Bay seashells and gold leaf flakes into hurricane candles that shone brightly, illuminated by a votive glass inside.

I was part of the assembly line. Mom would buy cases of really heavy wax sheets. My job was to haul the case out of the old Ford station wagon (with faux wood paneling) into the basement, where I was then tasked to use a clean hammer and break the sheets into small enough chunks to fit into the melting pots. To qualify for compensation, the wax had to be dirt free, my workplace had to be clean, and I had to make sure we did not run out of raw materials.

Mom would then apply her creativity to lay out the custom molds, insert the aforementioned seashells, driftwood, or other local jewels. Then it was time to melt the wax to just the right temperature, pour it carefully to ensure the decorations in the mold didn't move, and after cooldown and a short drum roll, a wax creation was born. Well, not quite.

After the wax cooled, it was Dad's turn. After a day of chasing spies in D.C. as an FBI foreign counterintelligence officer during the Cold War, Dad would put away his G-Man pistol and strap on his candle carving apron. Dad would move the "creation-in-process" to the other side of the basement, where his part of the assembly line was fit and finish.

Dad would take great care to remove the mold, which sometimes took great finesse because the wax would harden inside the grooves of the mold. He would then pull out his trusty carving knife and carefully trim all the wax from the mold lines. Once that was complete, Dad would plug in the trusty iron and eyeball the base of the candle. A candle that did not sit perfectly flat and balanced on the table was a reject, so Dad ironed the bottom of the creation until it sat proudly on the workbench. Once the carved and ironed creation was trimmed, it was submitted to the CEO of Chandelle (the French word for candle) for quality control review and approval.

In the next few days, one of the inventory distribution channels would be activated and I would play another pivotal role in client fulfillment. Candle distribution option number one was to drive the final product to the client's home. My job was to carefully load the double-boxed creation into the station wagon. Usually, the client delivery would coincide with sports or dance lessons so I would have to pack the box in between my sisters and our combined paraphernalia. Once we arrived at the client's home, Mom would carefully remove the inner box from the packing box and proudly deliver it to the new owner in exchange for the cold, hard cash.

Candle distribution option number two was the dreaded craft show.

Several times a year, we would spin up the production line to do "spec" work and create a bunch of inventory for the Blue Crab Festival or the annual Southern Maryland Jousting Tournament. These were especially trying times because not only did my factory work increase, but I had to tell my boys there would be no kick the can or bike riding for me that weekend.

My job was to strap on a good attitude and pack the inventory into the station wagon around my sisters and Twinkles. Upon arrival to the show site, I would unpack and deliver inventory and supplies under the direction of the craft show layout director / CEO / Mom. After the show setup was complete, as the oldest kid and worker bee, I did get a few privileges. I recall getting permission to walk around to meet the other vendors and explore their crafts. I still remember the "Duck Man," who carved wooden water fowl with precision. I saved up my commissions and eventually bought one I still have today.

Other than an enjoyable trip down memory lane for me, what does this have to do with rebuilding America?

Only everything.

The stuff we learn as kids that we don't even know we are learning has an incredible impact on our future. Our formative experiences have a huge influence on everyone we meet and our relationships. The impact of entrepreneurial accomplishment on my parents, siblings, and me went far beyond the money. I could write another book just on the lessons I learned as part of the family candle business, which expanded to antiques, T-shirts, and novelties. Those seeds were sown deep into my psyche. I wasn't just watching it on a TV reality show, I was living it. I didn't realize how much experience I was really getting. Being a laborer in the family candle business encouraged me to pursue my dreams while I was in school and ultimately for the rest of my life.

Here are a few questions to ponder:

What is the impact we can have on the next generation when we invite young people (not necessarily family members) to become an apprentice in our small business?

What is the value of teaching a work ethic that demonstrates how to take a calculated risk with a business idea that can create cash in hand?

Since there are tens of millions of young people who are unemployed right now, what would happen if 10, 20 or 100 kids in each American county learned and experienced small business?

My childhood memories along with more recent personal experiences would come flooding back to me some 35 years later as **The PATRIOT MISSION Story** began to take shape.

Chapter 4

Combat Flashback

In late 2010, I was finishing up a consulting project and transitioning from a business that had not gone nearly as well as I had hoped. There were a lot of stresses, financial challenges, and unfulfilled expectations. As I looked toward the New Year, a good friend and fellow small business consultant, Greg Land, and I began to discuss potential new projects. Since Greg was a legal resident from South Africa, he had a number of interesting perspectives about America.

We agreed the small business environment was getting tougher, not only because the economy was a shambles, but because the government and its shift to the left in 2008 was creating a number of new burdens on entrepreneurs. We began to discuss potential products and services to help small business owners.

Flashback: January 16, 2011

On the morning of January 16, 2011, I was sitting in my office reviewing some of the ideas Greg and I had discussed. We had rolled out a potential business model to a couple of colleagues and got a tepid response. At this point in my career, I was not interested in just doing another project to make money. Certainly the financial element was a consideration, but I wanted to do something that mattered. I remember leaning back in my executive chair and closing my eyes to quietly ask the Lord for some guidance. That was the moment everything changed.

Behind my chair in the office is a library table. On it sits an old-fashioned thing we call a radio with a stereo cassette player. At the top of the hour, the national news came on and the broadcaster mentioned the 20th anniversary of Desert Storm, a.k.a. the first Gulf War. I don't recall what else the announcer said, but I remember feeling like I got hit with a lightning strike.

As I sat in my leather chair, I was immediately transported back in time to Dhahran, Saudi Arabia in the middle of a cool January morning. I remember the feeling in my stomach the moment I heard the news. We had been called to a "Safety" meeting at our operations tent, which sat in the sand between the hardened bunkers where our F-15 Eagle fighter jets sat on alert. This "Safety" meeting was different because there were U.S. Air Force Security Policemen armed with machine guns standing outside the tent flaps and keeping everyone but the pilots out of earshot.

When the 27th Tactical Fighter Squadron Commander, Lt. Colonel Don "Karbo" Kline, was my age, he was flying F-4 Phantoms in Vietnam. A native Texan, he now sat in front of a bunch of young fighter pilots on a makeshift desk wearing his Lord Calvert baseball hat chewing a mouthful of Copenhagen tobacco. He looked over his shoulder at several big maps hanging from the tent's roof braces with the words **TOP SECRET** handwritten in bright red ink.

Karbo simply said: "*Gentlemen. Feed and water your horses, for tonight we ride.*"

Have you ever had a moment in your life when everything just stops?

You feel heavy pressure and have a hard time catching your breath. Everything that was normal 30 seconds ago is no longer so.

Karbo's announcement changed my world forever. In a few short hours, Desert Shield would become Operation Desert Storm. We were going to launch in the darkness and deliver a punch that would change warfare forever. This would be the first war broadcast on live TV. I wondered how Nancy would deal with it, in her eighth month of pregnancy.

Just to get to our jets, we had to dodge exploding SCUD and PATRIOT MISSILES fragments raining from the sky. Once airborne, we had to refuel in total silence and many times in nearly pitch black conditions. Once in hostile territory, our primary role was to lead the bombers into the danger zone and protect them while they found their targets. While we dodged the surface-to-air missiles and anti-aircraft artillery, we invited their fighter jets to tango. Suffice to say, when it came to air-to-air combat, the F-15 Eagle reigned supreme. This too could be another book, but just for the record:

U.S. Air Force F-15s – 35 | Iraqi Air Force – 0 | Enough said.

As a 26-year-old fighter pilot, I always believed Saddam Hussein would pull another rabbit out of his proverbial hat and stave off a full frontal attack from the most powerful, multi-national military force assembled in recent memory. I could not believe he would just stand aside and let the United States lead a coalition that would forcibly eject him from Kuwait and destroy his military.

I was wrong.

Here's why this flashback was so profound for me.

I sat in my office chair remembering how stunned I was that Saddam Hussein pridefully watched as we destroyed his military. Suddenly, I got an eerie feeling. Now 20 years later, I cannot believe I am watching the United States of America stand by and allow herself to be destroyed from within by its complacency, entitlement spirit, victim mentality, pathetic economics, growing disdain for capitalism, and historical ignorance.

I thought to myself, how can the mighty United States of America that I proudly served to free Kuwait from tyranny just stand by and let this happen? What is the world going to be like for my two baby girls and eventually their kids? At that very moment, I distinctly remember hearing these words from the still small voice inside me: "So what are YOU going to do about it?"

At first I thought, *"What do you mean, what am I going to do about it?"*

Then I quickly reconsidered. As a Christian, I have learned when God speaks to me it is a really good idea to listen. For a large part of my career I chose to do it my way and advise the Lord of my brilliant plans. (God needs a laugh, too.) That never worked out so well. I realized my quiet, prayerful pleas for clarity about the next steps in my work with Greg had just been answered.

Over the course of the next two years, **The PATRIOT MISSION Story** began to come to life.

From the very beginning it was clear our mission would be **To Rebuild America through the Power of Small Business**™. Interestingly, in 2005 I had purchased the website URL address www.PatriotMission.com and had never used it; must have been a coincidence (LOL).

The way I envision it, **The PATRIOT MISSION Story** has a happy ending.

It is a David and Goliath story of people who experienced or heard stories of what life used to be like in the USA and wondered why previous generations squandered it for them.

As we develop the storyline, we should consider a few compelling questions our kids and grandkids will likely ask us. These inquiries set the stage for the action sequence we get to write.

- Why did our parents borrow and blow trillions of dollars and then stick us with the tab?

- Whose brilliant idea was it to borrow money from the Chinese and give them all the leverage to control our economy, global resources, and trump our once powerful military?

- Did our parents not love us or were they just selfish?

- Why did the government steal our motivation to work by "giving" us food stamps, housing, health care, and free phones so we would quit being self-reliant and become totally dependent on the state?

- I thought our country was founded on biblical principles. When did you guys let the government decide the maker of the universe was no longer welcome in America?

- Once they figured out how bad the situation had become, was it too much trouble for our parents and grandparents to fight for us or were they just enjoying themselves too much to be bothered or worse yet, were they just too weak?

- Did our folks believe it was possible to solve their own problems or did they not understand what "WE THE PEOPLE" meant?

- If America was so great, why didn't someone stand up, wave the flag, and at least try to save the Republic so we could enjoy it, too?

Ouch. I don't even want to think about having to answer those questions, do you?

How does the storyline begin to take shape?

It begins with **7 Founding <u>LIBERTY</u> Principles** that are the PATRIOT MISSION bedrock.

If you are up for it, let's drill down into the core beliefs that motivate us to Rebuild America!

Chapter 5

7 Founding LIBERTY Principles

During my years as a military pilot, it was easy to define the enemy. Whoever violated our airspace, threatened to attack our homeland, or assaulted one of our allies was a bad guy. Before we strapped on our jets, we studied the rules of engagement and knew very clearly where the lines of demarcation were. Since 9/11/2001, those lines have become much more blurry. The United States has learned the hard way when you allow political correctness to permeate the society and you choose not to call out those whose expressed intention is to destroy you, it makes it exponentially more difficult to defend yourself.

In the years since I hung up my flight suit, it has become increasingly frustrating to watch so many Americans simply step back and voluntarily relinquish more and more of their freedoms. Do you ever wonder why they do so? Most Americans simply do not know our history. In 1905, George Santayana, a Spaniard living in America at the time wrote, *"Those who cannot remember the past are condemned to repeat it."* Those words are so true.

What do you believe about America? How did you come to your beliefs?

Those are important questions. I submit, few people have thought about or could answer them with certainty. Another challenge is many adults and an alarming number of younger

Americans do not understand basic civics or definitions of often used terms.

Here's an example. When we first launched PATRIOT MISSION, a number of well-meaning people challenged me on the use of the word patriot. *"That sounds like one of those right wing extremist groups."* To which I responded, "Really, how did you come to that conclusion? Do you know what the definition of the word patriot is?" Most people could not answer the questions. This is symptomatic of media power brokers who seek to control the language.

> DEFINITION: **Patriot**—*noun*—a person who loves, supports, and defends his or her country and its interests with devotion[2].

It's amazing how misled people can become when they are not encouraged to think. People actually believe: "If it is on TV or the Internet, it must be true." I asked a number of young people about how they confirm the validity of information they have read online or seen on TV.

What is their number one source for verification?

You probably guessed it; GOOGLE **search**. But interestingly, most said the search listing was sufficient as opposed to digging into the actual source documents or material from the search.

As you will see when we get into the tactical implementation of the blueprint, it is critical we begin with agreement on the basics. These **7 Founding LIBERTY Principles** are the basics for PATRIOT MISSION and should instill confidence for hope and optimism.

It is important to stress we do not expect nor are we encouraging the idea that we should be in agreement on everything. We want to have a healthy debate on a wide range of business issues, economic theories, leadership strategies, social concerns, and many other topics. However, these founding principles will not change; they are fundamental to our thinking and strategy.

My intention is to review each of the principles and give you some perspective on why they are important to us. By no means will this be an exhaustive discussion on these ideas. We created the acronym LIBERTY because it makes the principles easier to remember. Each letter in the word **LIBERTY** refers to the first letter of the key word in each principle.

> DEFINITION: **Liberty**—*noun*—freedom from arbitrary or despotic government or control[3].

LIBERTY Principle #1

We believe the economic Backbone of America™ is powered by the **LEADERSHIP** of Small Business Founders, employees, and their families.

Small business is often referred to as the Backbone of America™ because it drives such a large portion of our economy. In the vast majority of businesses, it is the founder who serves as the leader and sets the course for the company's growth and development. In order for a company to operate successfully, the first ingredient of success is the owner's personal leadership.

In my early business career I heard this saying: "Leader of one, leader of many. If you can't lead one, you can't lead any." This is so true, especially when it comes to expanding your staff. Your team wants you to lead. If I have employees, I will encourage them to grow to the best of their abilities as well. When they take responsibility for their own personal leadership and I empower them to do so, our small businesses can prosper.

In my opinion, one of the most overlooked and critical leadership segments that make or break an entrepreneur is their family support. This means there should be an intentional effort to nurture and recognize family leadership including spouses, children, and extended families. They need to know how their performance and support on the home front directly impacts the success of the company.

LIBERTY Principle #2

We believe providentially inspired American **INGENUITY** has created the strongest economy and most generous society the world has ever known.

As entrepreneurs, we get inspiration for our projects and businesses from a lot of places. It may be a perceived need in the marketplace or a customer suggestion. We know that our Founders and many others have described how "Providence" inspired their work including the Declaration of Independence. As Americans, we can define "Providence" however we see fit, but the key point is this level of inspiration leads to incredible creativity and ingenuity.

When you study World War II, specifically the industrial machine the U.S. created to fill the massive logistical needs for servicemen in two global theaters of operation, you will be amazed. This ingenuity spun off growth industries that powered our economy for decades.

Consider in 1961, when President Kennedy launched the Apollo project to launch men to the moon and to return them safely to Earth, the technology did not exist to complete that mission. American ingenuity funded by a booming postwar economy made that work.

The technology from the Apollo program alone created new industries in transportation, food safety, and non-perishable nutrition, which ultimately provided meals and medicine to millions of suffering people around the world. This is just one example of how inspired entrepreneurs who apply themselves fuel our economy and serve people around the globe.

Several of the latter LIBERTY principles describe the value, impact, and benefit of entrepreneurship in contrast with dependency that is encouraged by some local, state, and federal government programs. I want to make it very clear that a cornerstone of successful entrepreneurship is generosity both as a society and personally.

> *"From everyone who has been given much, much will be demanded; and from the one who has been entrusted with much, much more will be asked."*
> —Luke 12:48

There have been times in my life I would have crashed and burned had not my family, friends (many of whom were entrepreneurs), and my local church helped me. Not only did they help me financially in tough times, but they also mentored me and helped me get back on my feet. This type of community support, when effectively delivered, creates accountability and responsibility and does not diminish the self-esteem of the person who is being assisted.

Before many of the social welfare programs were started in the mid-twentieth century, local churches, synagogues, charity organizations, and neighbors took care of each other. That's the way it should be. Beyond that, having true safety net programs offered through responsible government is appropriate, but in my opinion should not be the primary support network.

There is a danger when government controls and dominates the distribution of resources; it can become a god of its own design.

LIBERTY Principle #3

We believe it is important to elect leaders who share a common **BELIEF** in our Judeo-Christian heritage and the magnificence of the U.S. Constitution.

I must admit this principle has created some controversy.

You may have guessed I have taken a few shots from people that want to school me on my arcane viewpoint. The funny part is when I explain what this means, most of the arguments disappear. It just goes to show how spring-loaded people are to automatically respond without any critical analysis.

Our principle does not say you have to be a Jew or a Christian to participate in PATRIOT MISSION programs. What we say is that you must believe in the Judeo-Christian heritage of America, which is the historical framework upon which the U.S. Constitution was founded. When you study the founding documents from a historically analytical perspective (as opposed to theological), our framer's viewpoint is indisputable.

This principle is really all about history. Judeo-Christian values are the basis for the U.S. Constitution, which stands on the premise that our rights come from God, not government. That means if we value the Constitution and our ability as "WE THE PEOPLE" to determine our future, then we must elect leaders who share that core belief.

As Americans, we are entitled to believe what we choose. There are plenty of organizations who are doing their best to erase God from our country's history and do not believe America should stand on her historical underpinnings. Regardless of your personal religious beliefs, if you do not agree with the fundamental values our Founders used to construct the Constitution, it is best for you to join another group.

LIBERTY Principle #4

We believe ENTREPRENEURSHIP is the primary economic means to inspire men and women to pursue their dreams and achieve prosperity.

Let's define this term. What is an entrepreneur?

DEFINITION: **Entrepreneur**—*noun*—a person who organizes and manages any enterprise, especially a business usually with considerable initiative and risk[4].

People who have never attempted to start a business cannot understand the intense emotion that is connected with entrepreneurship. Many times, as my mentor Michael Gerber says, it is an "Entrepreneurial Seizure" that launches people to go to work for themselves. It can also be the opportunity to pursue a passion, find a unique solution to a BIG problem, or reach a powerful, personal dream that motivates people to start a business.

However, an obvious and tremendous upside benefit to pursuing your dreams and solving problems through business is the opportunity to make money… potentially a lot of money. This can lead to economic prosperity if you do everything well. It can also be an economic disaster if you screw it up. I have personally experienced both sides of the equation and doing things well is much more enjoyable.

Entrepreneurs are willing to take the risk to pursue their providentially inspired dreams because they believe it is the right thing to do for them and because they believe prosperity will follow. When it does, everyone benefits including the clients, employees, investors, vendors, community, taxing authorities, and hopefully the owners themselves.

Contrast entrepreneurship with an alternative opportunity. Imagine if business rules stated you could pursue your dream by investing your capital after the government approves your plan. Then regardless of the profit, you only earn a bureaucratically approved salary and the title to your intellectual property is transferred to the government. These words describe this scenario in increasing degrees of intensity: socialism, Marxist Communism, and tyranny.

I choose entrepreneurship.

LIBERTY Principle #5

We believe Life, Liberty, and the Pursuit of Happiness are put at tremendous **RISK** by those who reject capitalism and promote excessive public spending.

> DEFINITION: **Capitalism**—*noun*—an economic system in which investment in and ownership of the means of production, distribution, and exchange of wealth is made and maintained chiefly by private individuals or corporations, esp. as contrasted to cooperatively or state-owned means of wealth[5].

This principle addresses the impact of public servants in elected, appointed, or employed bureaucratic positions of authority whose beliefs are contrary to the U.S. Constitution. When someone rejects capitalism, it is traditionally because they favor one of the previous varieties of utopian theory that have NEVER worked to grow and maintain a successful, robust economy.

Politicians on both sides of the aisle can be corrupted by the idea that government knows best, which is why it is critical to study the numbers. America is BROKE. At the time of this writing we have nearly 100 TRILLION DOLLARS in unfunded liabilities. We cannot spend what we do not have and to continue to do so is irresponsible, reprehensible, and is a direct threat to the only guarantee we have in the Constitution: Life, Liberty, and the Pursuit of Happiness.

I want to differentiate entrepreneurial or "grassroots capitalism," as I like to call it, with "Crony capitalism." In simple terms, when government does back door deals with companies who do not play by marketplace rules, they trash the system as well. This kind of back scratching, kickback-laden, crony deal-making infuriates those of us who play by the rules.

This is probably a good time to point out that PATRIOT MISSION (the company) is a for-profit business. We are not a political organization. We are not tied to any political party, candidate, PAC (political action committee), lobbying organization, or other affiliation. We study and discuss the political impact our elected officials have on our companies, families, and communities. We ask politicians hard questions and demand answers. We are not politically correct. We love capitalism and want to see it spread. That's the whole point of this work, which should be obvious by now.

LIBER_T_Y Principle #6

We believe Personal Property Rights and the Free Enterprise System are **TIMELESS** constitutional cornerstones upon which America was founded.

DEFINITION: **Free Enterprise**—*noun*—an economic and political doctrine holding that a capitalist economy can regulate itself in a freely competitive market through the relationship of supply and demand with a minimum of governmental intervention and regulation[6].

A cursory study of history proves the Free Enterprise system is amazingly successful, yet it is constantly demonized by senior bureaucrats and media personnel. Do you ever wonder why?

The answer is control and power. Successful entrepreneurs develop the skills to take an idea and turn it into income, profit, and equity. They have built their companies without wisdom from the intelligentsia. Why do we need government telling us what is best?

Answer… we don't. Therein lies the problem. The bureaucrats simply prefer business owners make money and give more of it to them so they can pass it out to those who they deem are worthy to receive it. The **overuse** of public assistance programs allows political elites to toot their own horns and lock in the loyalty of uninformed voters. Politicians give away products, services, and cash derived from those who produce results and fund the government via confiscatory regulatory fees and taxes.

This is a TIMELESS principle because it never changes. The God-breathed human spirit yearns to be free. That freedom includes the opportunity to make good and bad choices and reap the consequences from such decisions. Once a citizen owns property, which he has earned through the sweat of his brow (as opposed to government handouts), the inspiration to repeat the process and teach it to new generations continues.

Contrast this with the false doctrine of dependency and victimization. Think about the enormous human capital that sits in self-imposed bondage believing those who enslave them have their best interest at heart. It's similar to the constraints used to train elephants. Young elephants are tied to a stake and are not strong enough to escape. Even as they grow into powerful adults, once convinced they are too weak, they never break the ties that bind them.

LIBERT**Y** Principle #7

We believe it is crucial to inspire **YOUNG** citizens to become tough-minded, ethical entrepreneurs so they can help create long-term solutions for America.

The previous six principles lay out the case why America and her Constitution create an incredible opportunity for anyone who wants to apply themselves. At this point in our history, we must inspire our young people to pursue entrepreneurship.

In many cases, attending college, which used to be a standard path to prosperity, has been priced out of reach. Even in the cases where a student can borrow tens of thousands of dollars to attend college, one should ask what the return on investment is likely to be. A thorough examination of the numbers is crucial because many of our young people are leaving college with massive student loan debt hanging around their neck only to find there are few jobs.

The psychological impact on our younger generations is staggering. Worse yet, many young folks come to believe this is as good as it gets; the new normal. This thinking must be obliterated.

Here is one example to illustrate how our young people have an enormous advantage that is directly related to entrepreneurship. They are digital natives. The ability to leverage their technology skills creates a phenomenal opportunity to partner with seasoned business owners to fast track new ventures.

When strong mentoring is combined with education on the

other **LIBERTY** principles, our young people can quickly come to understand they are in a unique position to help us solve America's biggest challenges. It is important to do all we can to accelerate this knowledge because the young people are going to have to live with the consequences of our collective action or inaction.

I didn't realize the magnitude of what I was really learning when I was the young guy breaking wax, sweeping floors, packing boxes, and setting up craft fair display tables so my mom could sell candles. As my young career expanded, I worked for other entrepreneurs and tried my hand at a few of my own ventures. I got a deeper education as I learned how to mow lawns, shovel snow, pump gas, and dig ditches as a plumber's helper. I was blessed to live this LIBERTY principle and believe if I had not been inspired by my mom and dad's candle business, **The PATRIOT MISSION Story** may never have been written.

As you can see, these principles serve as a solid foundation upon which we can stand together in agreement. Once we have this agreement, we know where each other stands. These principles serve as standards which guide and direct our way of doing business and making decisions.

Just for the record, as long as we can agree on these seven principles, we can keep moving forward. If not, let's agree to disagree and part company now.

The next few segments of the storyline will introduce the fast moving action sequences. This is the fun part. I like to think of these storyline scenes in flying terms. The **7 Founding LIBERTY Principles** are analogous to the unchanging laws of physics, the theory of flight, and the mechanical parts that make our jet work.

Let's learn how to strap on our jet, kick in 10 stages of afterburner, do a vertical takeoff, and accelerate into the heavens to engage our adversaries with successful entrepreneurship. As we feel the power and strength of these three words: **LEAD, BUILD,** and **GROW,** our revolutionary dream roars to life.

Chapter 6

"The Shining City on a Hill"

In the late 1970s, there were a number of major events happening in the United States and around the world. Only a few years earlier, the Watergate scandal led to the resignation of a United States President. I can still remember sitting with my dad in his home office listening to President Richard Nixon on the radio announcing his departure. I can still see the painful look of disappointment on my dad's face. Dad looked at me and told me it was a sad day for America.

Vice President Gerald Ford succeeded Nixon in 1974. Interestingly, in 1973 Gerald Ford was appointed to replace Vice President Spiro Agnew, after he resigned as a result of being charged with bribery and other felonious activity. Ford was unique because he was the only chief executive to have never been elected as America's President or Vice President. He served out the balance of Nixon's term and lost to Jimmy Carter in 1976. All of this political chaos played out as the Vietnam War was winding down.

Carter came into office with a focused effort to try to get the country back on track. Unfortunately, his strategy did not work. Under the Carter Administration the economy became a wreck. Home mortgage rates soared to over 20% with inflation in the mid-teens. If you have a mortgage now, run the numbers and see what your payment would be at a 20% interest rate and you will get an idea of how depressing things were in the good ole' US of A.

I don't want to debate the political element that drove these situations.

Rather, I want to focus on the mood of the country. It was awful. In 1977, I got my first real job at a local gas station. As a 13-year-old kid, I learned to pump gas, wash windows, and answer the phone properly. I also learned how to become a traffic cop and keep people away from the pumps because we had to ration gas. People got into fistfights because they needed gas and we couldn't sell it to them.

One of the darkest days in U.S. history was November 4, 1979, when the American Embassy in Tehran was attacked and our diplomats were taken hostage. You may have seen the 2012 film Argo. It told the story of six hostages who managed to escape in the early days of the crisis and their incredible rescue. In April 1980, there was a failed rescue attempt that cost the lives of eight servicemen. America seemed paralyzed, Iran was calling the shots, and our Cold War foe, the Soviet Union was turning up the heat against us in many of its satellite countries.

Then things began to change. In the fall of 1980, I turned 16 and Ronald Reagan was elected President of the United States. Reagan was a renegade. He was a former Hollywood actor and California Governor. There was a cautious optimism that began to develop, most of which I didn't understand because I wasn't following politics. I just remember listening to my folks, speaking with grownups at the gas station and at my high school. People seemed to be encouraged and hopeful.

My dad recalled the day after the 1980 election walking on the streets of Washington, D.C. and experiencing a rare situation. Complete strangers were smiling, shaking hands, and telling each other that things were going to be OK. In his 40 years working in D.C., the day after the Redskins won the Super Bowl was the only other time Dad saw this type of jubilation on the streets.

On the day President Reagan was inaugurated, January 20, 1981, 444 days after the Iranian embassy siege began, at the exact moment he concluded his first address to the nation, all the hostages were released. That was the dawn of a new day in America. Regardless of your position on his politics, President Reagan told an American story that brought us together.

He communicated an inspiring appreciation and reverence for our nation and he led the country without apology. The fact he won a 49 state landslide in his 1984 reelection bid is testament to how the American people felt about him and the direction he was taking the country. The brutal division in our land was finally healing.

What does this have to do with rebuilding America today, nearly two and a half decades later?

President Reagan showed us what is possible in the face of a divided and depressed country. He tapped into the spirit of our Founders and the uniqueness that makes us Americans. Reagan recognized there were many differing opinions, many of which emanated from his own party. At the end of the day, Reagan listened to his staff, weighed his options against the supremacy of the U.S. Constitution, made his decisions, and stood by them. President Reagan wasn't perfect. No man is. He was an outstanding leader, encourager, and communicator.

Even as a young man, I can remember feeling encouraged. I had never heard the term "American Exceptionalism" but I felt it. As I graduated from high school in 1982, the recession was ending and the economy was booming. The first of the Reagan era's 19,000,000 jobs were being created.

In the Spring of 1986, as the cadet commander of the U.S. Air Force ROTC Detachment 330 at the University of Maryland, I wrote President Reagan a letter asking him to officiate at our graduation. Although it was his standard practice to only attend one commencement a year, rotating between the military academies, I decided to write anyway. My parents had always told me I could do anything I put my mind to, so I gave it a shot.

Unfortunately, his schedule didn't permit him to join us. As a consolation prize, President Reagan signed my commission as a Second Lieutenant. As a bonus, the weekend I graduated in 1986, TOP GUN hit the theaters and I began to get fired up and focused on heading to undergraduate pilot training in Phoenix, Arizona. Life was good.

In my research, I spoke with many people who only vaguely remembered, if at all, President Reagan's speeches or his references to the "Shining City on a Hill." Obviously, many of our young people were not born or were just toddlers back then. There is a reason he was called "The Great Communicator"; his words were powerful.

Originally, I only planned to share the last couple paragraphs of President Reagan's Farewell Address to the Nation on January 11, 1989. However, as I read it from the beginning, it brought back many positive memories and lit my fire. As you take in his words, imagine the possibilities of inspiring a new generation.

Ponder the potential when tens of thousands of leaders who stand with us on our **7 LIBERTY Principles** share a similar passion as our 40th President. As he describes the shining city, see it in your mind's eye begin to emerge from beneath the dark clouds that suffocate it now. Together, we can Rebuild America!

President Reagan's Farewell Address to the Nation[1]

January 11, 1989
My fellow Americans:

This is the 34th time I'll speak to you from the Oval Office and the last. We've been together 8 years now, and soon it'll be time for me to go. But before I do, I wanted to share some thoughts, some of which I've been saving for a long time.

It's been the honor of my life to be your President. So many of you have written the past few weeks to say thanks, but I could say as much to you. Nancy and I are grateful for the opportunity you gave us to serve.

One of the things about the Presidency is that you're always somewhat apart. You spend a lot of time going by too fast in a car someone else is driving, and seeing the people through tinted glass—the parents holding up a child, and the wave you saw too late and couldn't return. And so many times I wanted to stop and reach out from behind the glass, and connect. Well, maybe I can do a little of that tonight.

People ask how I feel about leaving. And the fact is, "parting is such sweet sorrow." The sweet part is California and the ranch and freedom. The sorrow—the goodbyes, of course, and leaving this beautiful place.

You know, down the hall and up the stairs from this office is the part of the White House where the President and his family live. There are a few favorite windows I have up there that I like to stand and look out of early in the morning. The view is over the grounds here to the Washington Monument, and then the Mall and the Jefferson Memorial. But on mornings when the humidity is low, you can see past the Jefferson to the river, the Potomac, and the Virginia shore. Someone said that's the view Lincoln had when he saw the smoke rising from the Battle of Bull Run. I see more prosaic things: the grass on the banks, the morning traffic as people make their way to work, now and then a sailboat on the river.

I've been thinking a bit at that window. I've been reflecting on what the past 8 years have meant and mean. And the image that comes to mind like a refrain is a nautical one—a small story about a big ship, and a refugee, and a sailor. It was back in the early eighties, at the height of the boat people. And the sailor was hard at work on the carrier Midway, which was patrolling the South China Sea. The sailor, like most American servicemen, was young, smart, and fiercely observant. The crew spied on the horizon a leaky little boat. And crammed inside were refugees from Indochina hoping to get to America. The Midway sent a small launch to bring them to the ship and safety. As the refugees made their way through the choppy seas, one spied the sailor on deck, and stood up, and called out to him. He yelled, "Hello, American sailor. Hello, freedom man."

A small moment with a big meaning, a moment the sailor, who wrote it in a letter, couldn't get out of his mind. And, when I saw it, neither could I. Because that's what it was to be an American in the 1980s. We stood, again, for freedom. I know we always have, but in the past few years the world again—and in a way, we ourselves—rediscovered it.

It's been quite a journey this decade, and we held together through some stormy seas. And at the end, together, we are reaching our destination.

The fact is, from Grenada to the Washington and Moscow summits, from the recession of '81 to '82, to the expansion that began in late '82 and continues to this day, we've made a difference. The way I see it, there were two great triumphs, two things that I'm proudest of. One is the economic recovery, in which the people of America created—and filled—19 million new jobs. The other is the recovery of our morale. America is respected again in the world and looked to for leadership.

Something that happened to me a few years ago reflects some of this. It was back in 1981, and I was attending my first big economic summit, which was held that year in Canada. The meeting place rotates among the member countries. The opening meeting was a formal dinner for the heads of government of the seven industrialized nations. Now, I sat there like the new kid in school and listened, and it was all Francois this and Helmut that. They dropped titles and spoke to one another on a first-name basis. Well, at one point I sort of leaned in and said, "My name's Ron." Well, in that same year, we began the actions we felt would ignite an economic comeback—cut taxes and regulation, started to cut spending. And soon the recovery began.

Two years later, another economic summit with pretty much the same cast. At the big opening meeting we all got together, and all of a sudden, just for a moment, I saw that everyone was just sitting there looking at me. And then one of them broke the silence. *"Tell us about the American miracle,"* he said.

Well, back in 1980, when I was running for President, it was all so different. Some pundits said our programs would result in catastrophe. Our views on foreign affairs would cause war. Our plans for the economy would cause inflation to soar and bring about economic collapse. I even remember one highly respected economist saying, back in 1982, that "The engines of economic growth have shut down here, and they're likely to stay that way for years to come." Well, he and the other opinion leaders were wrong. The fact is, what they called "radical" was really "right." What they called "dangerous" was just "desperately needed."

And in all of that time I won a nickname, "The Great Communicator." But I never thought it was my style or the words I used that made a difference: it was the content. I wasn't a great communicator, but I communicated great things, and they didn't spring full bloom from my brow, they came from the heart of a great nation—from our experience, our wisdom, and our belief in the principles that have guided us for two centuries. They called it the Reagan Revolution. Well, I'll accept that, but for me it always seemed more like the great rediscovery, a rediscovery of our values and our common sense.

Common sense told us that when you put a big tax on something, the people will produce less of it. So, we cut the people's tax rates, and the people produced more than ever before. The economy bloomed like a plant that had been cut back and could now grow quicker and stronger. Our economic program brought about the longest peacetime expansion in our history: real family income up, the poverty rate down, entrepreneurship booming, and an explosion in research and new technology. We're exporting more than ever because American industry became more competitive and at the same time, we summoned the national will to knock down protectionist walls abroad instead of erecting them at home.

Common sense also told us that to preserve the peace, we'd have to become strong again after years of weakness and confusion. So, we rebuilt our defenses, and this New Year we toasted the new peacefulness around the globe. Not only have the superpowers actually begun to reduce their stockpiles of nuclear weapons—and hope for even more progress is bright—but the regional conflicts that wrack the globe are also beginning to cease. The Persian Gulf is no longer a war zone. The Soviets are leaving Afghanistan. The Vietnamese are preparing to pull out of Cambodia, and an American-mediated accord will soon send 50,000 Cuban troops home from Angola.

The lesson of all this was, of course, that because we're a great nation, our challenges seem complex. It will always be this way. But as long as we remember our first principles and believe in ourselves, the future will always be ours. And something else we learned: Once you begin a great movement, there's no telling where it will end. We meant to change a nation, and instead, we changed a world.

Countries across the globe are turning to free markets and free speech and turning away from the ideologies of the past. For them, the great rediscovery of the 1980s has been that, lo and behold, the moral way of government is the practical way of government: Democracy, the profoundly good, is also the profoundly productive.

When you've got to the point when you can celebrate the anniversaries of your 39th birthday, you can sit back sometimes, review your life, and see it flowing before you. For me there was a fork in the river, and it was right in the middle of my life. I never meant to go into politics. It wasn't my intention when I was young. But I was raised to believe you had to pay your way for the blessings bestowed on you. I was happy with my career in the entertainment world, but I ultimately went into politics because I wanted to protect something precious.

Ours was the first revolution in the history of mankind that truly reversed the course of government, and with three little words: "We the People." "We the People" tell the government what to do; it doesn't tell us. "We the People" are the driver; the government is the car. And we decide where it should go, and by what route, and how fast. Almost all the world's constitutions are documents in which governments tell the people what their privileges are. Our Constitution is a document in which "We the People" tell the government what it is allowed to do. "We the People" are free. This belief has been the underlying basis for everything I've tried to do these past 8 years.

But back in the 1960s, when I began, it seemed to me that we'd begun reversing the order of things—that through more and more rules and regulations and confiscatory taxes, the government was taking more of our money, more of our options, and more of our freedom. I went into politics in part to put up my hand and say, "Stop." I was a citizen politician, and it seemed the right thing for a citizen to do.

I think we have stopped a lot of what needed stopping. And I hope we have once again reminded people that man is not free unless government is limited. There's a clear cause and effect here that is as neat and predictable as a law of physics: As government expands, liberty contracts.

Nothing is less free than pure communism—and yet we have, the past few years, forged a satisfying new closeness with the Soviet Union. I've been asked if this isn't a gamble, and my answer is no because we're basing our actions not on words but deeds. The detente of the 1970s was based not on actions but promises. They'd promise to treat their own people and the people of the world better. But the gulag was still the gulag, and the state was still expansionist, and they still waged proxy wars in Africa, Asia, and Latin America.

Well, this time, so far, it's different. President Gorbachev has brought about some internal democratic reforms and begun the withdrawal from Afghanistan. He has also freed prisoners whose names I've given him every time we've met.

But life has a way of reminding you of big things through small incidents. Once, during the heady days of the Moscow summit, Nancy and I decided to break off from the entourage one afternoon to visit the shops on Arbat Street—that's a little street just off Moscow's main shopping area. Even though our visit was a surprise, every Russian there immediately recognized us and called out our names and reached for our hands. We were just about swept away by the warmth. You could almost feel the possibilities in all that joy. But within seconds, a KGB detail pushed their way toward us and began pushing and shoving the people in the crowd. It was an interesting moment. It reminded me that while the man on the street in the Soviet Union yearns for peace, the government is Communist. And those who run it are Communists, and that means we and they view such issues as freedom and human rights very differently.

We must keep up our guard, but we must also continue to work together to lessen and eliminate tension and mistrust. My view is that President Gorbachev is different from previous Soviet leaders. I think he knows some of the things wrong with his society and is trying to fix them. We wish him well. And we'll continue to work to make sure that the Soviet Union that eventually emerges from this process is a less threatening one. What it all boils down to is this: I want the new closeness to continue. And it will, as long as we make it clear that we will continue to act in a certain way as long as they continue to act in a helpful manner. If and when they don't, at first pull your punches. If they persist, pull the plug. It's still trust but verify. It's still play, but cut the cards. It's still watch closely. And don't be afraid to see what you see.

I've been asked if I have any regrets. Well, I do. The deficit is one. I've been talking a great deal about that lately, but tonight isn't for arguments, and I'm going to hold my tongue. But an observation: I've had my share of victories in the Congress, but what few people noticed is that I never won anything you didn't win for me. They never saw my troops, they never saw Reagan's regiments, the American people. You won every battle with every call you made and letter you wrote demanding action. Well, action is still needed. If we're to finish the job, Reagan's regiments will have to become the Bush brigades. Soon he'll be the chief, and he'll need you every bit as much as I did.

Finally, there is a great tradition of warnings in Presidential farewells, and I've got one that's been on my mind for some time. But oddly enough it starts with one of the things I'm proudest of in the past 8 years: the resurgence of national pride that I called the new patriotism. This national feeling is good, but it won't count for much, and it won't last unless it's grounded in thoughtfulness and knowledge.

An informed patriotism is what we want. And are we doing a good enough job teaching our children what America is and what she represents in the long history of the world? Those of us who are over 35 or so years of age grew up in a different America. We were taught, very directly, what it means to be an American. And we absorbed, almost in the air, a love of country and an appreciation of its institutions. If you didn't get these things from your family you got them from the neighborhood, from the father down the street who fought in Korea, or the family who lost someone at Anzio. Or you could get a sense of patriotism from school. And if all else failed you could get a sense of patriotism from the popular culture. The movies celebrated democratic values and implicitly reinforced the idea that America was special. TV was like that, too, through the mid-sixties.

But now, we're about to enter the nineties, and some things have changed. Younger parents aren't sure that an unambivalent appreciation of America is the right thing to teach modern children. And as for those who create the popular culture, well-grounded patriotism is no longer the style. Our spirit is back, but we haven't reinstitutionalized it. We've got to do a better job of getting across that America is freedom—freedom of speech, freedom of religion, freedom of enterprise. And freedom is special and rare. It's fragile; it needs production [protection].

So, we've got to teach history based not on what's in fashion but what's important—why the Pilgrims came here, who Jimmy Doolittle was, and what those 30 seconds over Tokyo meant. You know, 4 years ago on the 40th anniversary of D-Day, I read a letter from a young woman writing to her late father, who'd fought on Omaha Beach. Her name was Lisa Zanatta Henn, and she said, "We will always remember, we will never forget what the boys of Normandy did." Well, let's help her keep her word. If we forget what we did, we won't know who we are. I'm warning of an eradication of the American memory that could result, ultimately, in an erosion of the American spirit. Let's start with some basics: more attention to American history and a greater emphasis on civic ritual.

And let me offer lesson number one about America: All great change in America begins at the dinner table. So, tomorrow night in the kitchen I hope the talking begins. And children, if your parents haven't been teaching you what it means to be an American, let 'em know and nail 'em on it. That would be a very American thing to do.

And that's about all I have to say tonight, except for one thing. The past few days when I've been at that window upstairs, I've thought a bit of the "shining city upon a hill." The phrase comes from John Winthrop, who wrote it to describe the America he imagined. What he imagined was important because he was an early Pilgrim, an early freedom man. He journeyed here on what today we'd call a little wooden boat; and like the other Pilgrims, he was looking for a home that would be free.

I've spoken of the shining city all my political life, but I don't know if I ever quite communicated what I saw when I said it. But in my mind it was a tall, proud city built on rocks stronger than oceans, wind-swept, God-blessed, and teeming with people of all kinds living in harmony and peace; a city with free ports that hummed with commerce and creativity. And if there had to be city walls, the walls had doors and the doors were open to anyone with the will and the heart to get here. That's how I saw it, and see it still.

And how stands the city on this winter night? More prosperous, more secure, and happier than it was 8 years ago. But more than that: After 200 years, two centuries, she still stands strong and true on the granite ridge, and her glow has held steady no matter what storm. And she's still a beacon, still a magnet for all who must have freedom, for all the pilgrims from all the lost places who are hurtling through the darkness, toward home.

We've done our part. And as I walk off into the city streets, a final word to the men and women of the Reagan Revolution, the men and women across America who for 8 years did the work that brought America back. My friends: We did it. We weren't just marking time. We made a difference. We made the city stronger, we made the city freer, and we left her in good hands. All in all, not bad, not bad at all.

And so, good-bye, God bless you, and God bless the United States of America.

Note: The President spoke at 9:02 p.m. from the Oval Office at the White House. The address was broadcast live on nationwide radio and television.

Right now in America, we are experiencing a similar time as the late 1970s and early 1980s (much worse in some ways). America has a massive leadership deficit, a horrendous national debt, worsening unemployment, a shaky economy with irresponsible budget deficits, terrorists hitting our homeland and political correctness run amok. Our cultural and social problems are ugly. Worst of all, God has largely been dismissed from the public square as well as private institutions. Left unchecked, these factors and many others will continue to drive us into a very dark place and in my opinion, beyond the point of no return.

How do we leverage President Reagan's stunning word picture of the "Shining City on a Hill" in our storyline?

Step one is to recognize how quickly the power of history can escape from our personal and national memory. If you were alive during the Reagan era, I will wager a good cup of coffee that as you relived his speech, it brought back good memories about the strength and power of America when she was at the top of her game.

America and her foundational values are ideas that need to be lived, experienced, honored, and enjoyed every day. It starts with leaders who are good students of history. The past comes alive with mountaintop learning experiences or field trips as we called them in elementary school. We can combine lessons learned from outings with self study and apply these insights in our daily lives.

The Reagan Revolution ushered in the rebirth of a vibrant, modern America. History can and will repeat itself. America does not have time to sit back and wait for one elected person to come to the rescue. We need to be inspired and begin an entrepreneurial revolution to reduce the lines of division between artificially segmented people groups. We must plant these "freedom" seeds in every corner of the nation so we can start to Rebuild America... and we can have fun doing it.

The PATRIOT MISSION Story will become stronger as we recruit the group of founding partners who see what President Reagan saw when he described the "Shining City on a Hill." When we rediscover the beauty that is our founding and the power of God's hand on our nation, then we can humbly submit ourselves to the important work before us.

When we LEAD our fellow Americans to Rediscover the "Shining City on a Hill" (or perhaps discover for the first time), we will ignite a positively infectious American Spirit and inspire a new generation to see the possibilities just like President Reagan did for us three decades ago.

We can do this, if we believe we can.

I believe we can.

PART II

HOW CAN WE REBUILD AMERICA?

"I believe this nation should commit itself to achieving the goal of putting a man on the moon before this decade is out."

– John F. Kennedy –

Chapter 7

BUILD Bold Leadership Teams in Every County, City, and Parish

In these next few chapters, we are going to move from the big picture down into the practical opportunities that will have a fantastic impact in your local area. You may even start to get nervous. It may sound like I am going to ask you to get out of your comfort zone. No need for paranoia. As we walk through this, I believe you'll be pleasantly surprised. I will encourage you to focus on what you do best and challenge you to inspire Americans in your area. There are millions of our fellow citizens who need to be inspired, encouraged, and led right now.

After you have a powerful breakthrough, either personally or professionally, how do you feel?

Once you have a breakthrough experience, you typically have a paradigm shift. You see things in a whole new way. Your frame of reference changes and typically, you become much bolder about sharing your point of view. If you are an entrepreneur or small business owner, think back to a breakthrough in your company... a moment in time when everything changed for you.

What happened to your intensity about your vision? Did you shrivel up and become meek or did you feel strong, confident, and bold as you took your ideas to the streets?

What do you think will happen when tens of thousands of citizens learn about the America they never knew existed? Fellow Americans will discover our nation is the only one on the planet founded on principles specifically designed to empower them to pursue life as they choose with unparalleled opportunity. **The PATRIOT MISSION Story** will welcome tens of thousands of people to plug in and apply these ideas in their own lives in order to pursue their American Dream. Think about the unbridled energy that will be unleashed on the marketplace.

> DEFINITION: **American Dream**—*noun*—the ideals of freedom, equality, and opportunity traditionally held to be available to every American[7].

Do you think people are going to get this message through traditional media or news channels?

Not likely.

The only way this message will ever make it to the grassroots level of America is when those of us who have experienced or understand the power of small business make time to share it with others. It will only happen when leaders emboldened by our own beliefs about the goodness of the USA decide to take action and help our fellow citizens discover the "Shining City on a Hill."

The reason millions of Americans are ready to hear this message is because they are beginning to realize a government sponsored recovery is not coming. Most people do not understand or care about macro or micro economic theories. They do understand their checkbooks and savings accounts. There are millions of people who truly want to work and contribute to their families, companies, and communities at large. The problem is they have been convinced there is nothing they can do to change their future. They are told to stand in line and deal with *"the new normal."*

That is a BOLDFACE LIE.

Granted, there are many millions of people who do prefer to let you and me work our butts off and transfer our cash to them through lifelong entitlement programs. Those people do not have ears to hear our message right now. Some may never want to hear it because it will mean they have to get off the couch and become productive citizens. Unfortunately, like a spoiled child, this complacency factor has infected many people with sloth and entitlement syndrome.

Previously, I mentioned our strategy is designed to impact multiple generations. Once the first round of newly inspired Americans begins to understand the power of small business and the joy of taking an idea from concept to cash, they will be the ones to inspire some who have chosen to stay behind. Unfortunately, many will choose to stay behind and wither on the vine. That must not keep us from our work. Still others who face obstacles other than laziness will need to be served by our churches, communities, and government safety net programs, but hopefully not forever.

I was blessed to have parents that told me I could do anything I put my mind to. Whether that meant becoming an Air Force pilot, owning an international company, or living in a trash dumpster, the choice was mine to make. One of the most shocking discoveries I have made during my career has been the number of people who were never encouraged to succeed by their family and friends. It wasn't just the fact they were not encouraged; many were actually told to quit trying to make something of themselves because they would never succeed. Parents would ask: "*Who do you think you are?*" One guy told me his family continually drummed this refrain:

"YOU ARE A LOSER.... and YOU WILL ALWAYS BE A LOSER."

How's that for encouragement?

Here's a little nature story to illustrate why I think so many people have never been encouraged.

Growing up in Maryland was a great experience. In the late '70s and early '80s there was a private retreat near Solomon's Island called The Chesapeake Ranch Club. One of the benefits of my parents' candle business was the cash they saved to buy a lot in the club, which was a requirement to join. It was a little slice of heaven about an hour south of Washington, D.C. We could escape the busy life of metro D.C. to ride horses on trails, fire a few rounds at the shooting range, fly fish for bass or bluegill on Lake Lariat, or go to the private beach on the Chesapeake Bay.

Over the years, one of the fun adventures we enjoyed was to invite our friends to join us for a crab feast. If you've never had this experience, you should put it on your bucket list. When you buy a bushel of live crabs, you may notice an interesting phenomenon. Every now and again, one of the soon-to-be-lunch critters decides to make a break for it. The escape artist will try to get out of the bushel basket. Usually you don't have to chase him down because one of the other less industrious crabs will reach up and grab the one trying to get out. The crab who has already accepted his fate tells the escapee that if he has to stay in the bushel, so does everyone else.

Sadly, this line of thinking is prevalent in America today. When our fellow citizens attempt to escape the bondage of dependency on low wage or fixed government income, many times their friends or family pull them right back into the bushel. Sometimes the friend is well meaning and doesn't want the person to get hurt by thinking about raising their personal game. Other times it is the painful influence of decade's long dependency that paralyzes people and speaks fear into the lives of those who would break out. There are a lot of people who don't have the guts to reach for the stars and would rather see everyone else stay in the bushel with them.

This is precisely why leaders need to step up to speak truth, encouragement, and facilitate opportunity into the lives of fellow Americans all across our land.

To give you a perspective of the impact we can have, let's look at a simple example. We will keep the numbers very small and focused on an average U.S. County. How hard do you think it would it be to find 100 folks in an average county who would agree with our **7 <u>LIBERTY</u> Principles**? I am confident we could find 100 like-minded people among the small business owners, entrepreneurs, community economic development supporters, and start-up founders.

Suppose once a month, we met at a local leadership development event and each of us invested 20 minutes encouraging three people who wanted to learn about entrepreneurship. That's 100 leaders sharing stories, face to face, with 300 apprentices who desperately want to believe they can tap into the potential buried deep inside them. Each successive month we rotate and have the opportunity to mentor three more fellow Americans. We get to share our story and learn theirs.

Where could we find 300 prospective apprentices who might be interested in entrepreneurship?

The weak economy has had a devastating impact on young people coming out of high school and many others on career development pathways. Depending on which statistics you believe, the American workforce is smaller than it was back in the Carter Administration. Again, without delving into all the geopolitical reasons for the economic disaster, let's focus on the people who want to work, what they are doing to get by now, and how our leadership team could help them.

Do you know any college students who graduated, perhaps with sizable, government-managed student loans, only to discover there are no jobs available? Many sheepishly come back home and live with their parents while they continue to try to find work. Young people I know want to work. Depending on the geographic location, many young people have had to compete for minimum wage jobs with formerly retired senior citizens who had to go back to work.

What about downsized employees whose companies cannot afford to pay them what they used to earn due to increased taxes and the new costs of health care? Then there are the single parent families whose taxes have gone up and now need extra money to make ends meet. We also have the under-employed people who are working, but not in their field of choice or expertise, which would command a higher income. These people want to work and be productive members of society. They have no interest in eating at the public trough.

Right now, what do people in these cash flow challenged situations do to cover their most basic needs? If they don't have a church, family or friends who can help, many are forced to apply for government assistance programs like food stamps. They don't want to, but at the end of the day after pounding the pavement, sending out résumés, and doing all they can to find work, they need to eat and make sure they have shelter. This is how safety net programs are supposed to be used. Most Americans are happy to help those less fortunate.

How many folks facing these types of challenges do you think live in your county?

I know we could find at least 300 fellow Americans in your area who would love to meet with successful entrepreneurs, small business owners, and sole proprietors to learn about their experiences. We are confident people from all walks of life will stand in line to engage in mentoring relationships with supportive people who want to see the local economy grow.

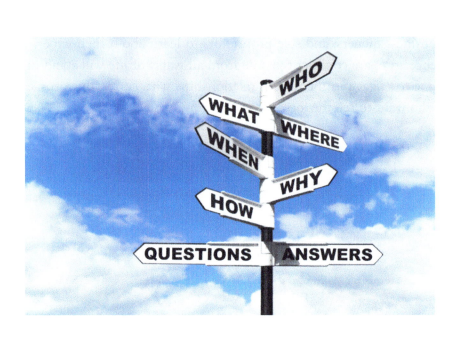

Chapter 8

Mentorship—A Turning Point Toward the Future

Mentorship can make a powerful, lifelong impact. You may have experienced mentoring on the giving or receiving end. Let me share an experience I had with a mentor who helped me.

After I graduated from college in 1986, I was technically an Air Force officer, but I was not yet on active duty, which means I was not getting paid. I had to wait almost 10 months for my pilot training start date in Phoenix. While I got my mind ready for the grueling 49 week course that typically washes out 50% of the students, I was keeping busy working several jobs. I still had the gas station job where I first worked at the age of 13 and also the spinoff laborer job I got as a plumber's helper digging ditches and keeping the master craftsmen loaded with supplies.

One of the jobs I added to my résumé toward the end of college was door-to-door canvasser. Due to all the freaks out there now, these jobs have largely gone away. We were the guys who would knock on your door during dinner to deliver the remarkable news that your windows and siding were incredibly close to falling off your house. "Fortunately for you, Mr. Homeowner, we just happen to have a gifted pitchman scheduled to be in your neighborhood tomorrow so why don't we schedule an appointment?"

Most times when Harry Homeowner answered the front door in a wife beater T-shirt with hamburger hanging out of his face, he didn't much care to hear what I had to say. I didn't mind hard work, but I preferred to do something somewhat more productive. After interrupting 1000 family dinners, I decided to pursue greener pastures.

I had gotten a tip about a much better deal to work as a window washer, gutter cleaner, and chimney sweep. What a bonus. Three gigs in one. So I loaded up my 1968 Barracuda convertible with portable ladders, buckets, trash bags, chimney brushes, soap, and hoses. For the next few months I traveled around the D.C. Beltway into the more fashionable parts of Maryland, Virginia and the District of Columbia, where people would actually pay me to do stuff they didn't want to do on a Saturday afternoon.

This is where I started to observe the benefits of entrepreneurship.

I would ask the homeowners what they did and many of them were business owners. It wasn't worth their time to do the work they paid me to do. I liked the idea of being in the easy chair paying someone to do the work. At the end of the cleanup, many times they would offer me a beverage and tell me their story. While most of the stories did not include flying jets, I enjoyed learning about their business ventures. It didn't take long to get my fill of hour-long traffic jams and the potential career ending dangers of standing on top of a 25-foot ladder climbing on wet, slate roofs and chimneys.

I got an idea. I called a friend of my parents who was an Air Force pilot in our neighborhood. My sisters were friends with his kids and he was one of my lawn mowing clients years before. He had been stationed at Andrews in the 89th Airlift Squadron which flies the President, government officials, and other dignitaries who enjoy taxpayer funded travel. This gentleman left the military after a relatively short career to pursue a real estate business. I was fascinated to learn more about his experience both as an Air Force pilot and a blossoming real estate mogul.

Although I was nervous, I made the phone call and asked if I could take him to lunch and pick his brain. He said yes and I was excited. We scheduled our meeting after the 4th of July, 1986. That was a special weekend because I was on my way to New York City to celebrate the 100th Anniversary of the Statue of Liberty. It was a great opportunity to learn about the gift from the French and how Lady Liberty landed in New York Harbor. OK, I admit at 21 years old it was a boondoggle to the Big Apple. Looking back on it, there was a good amount of educational value and an awesome fireworks display.

Upon returning to Maryland, sporting a nice bankroll from my laborer jobs, I stepped up and took my soon-to-be mentor to McDonalds. In our meeting Dennis told me his story of working real estate between his Air Force trips. He also explained to me why traveling around the world flying cargo / people haulers would be much more fun than flying fighters. Travel is great, but I learned flying supersonic with your hair on fire beats hours of boredom boring holes in the sky.

The biggest development from the meeting was Dennis hired me for a fourth job.

Every Saturday and Sunday for the next eight months until I left for flight school, I would assist his VP of Sales, Mark "Doc" Daugherty at his model townhome sales office. As it turned out, I learned more from Doc about marketing, sales, and jazz music in those eight months than I could have ever imagined. Doc became a mentor, coach, friend, business partner, and lifelong confidant until he went home to be with the Lord in 2011.

I had no idea that a one hour lunch meeting in the summer of 1986 would change the direction of my life. I can trace back many of the decisions I made throughout my military and business careers to specific events that were a direct result of that single meeting. You just never know what will happen when you ask someone for help and you are willing to listen to the answers.

What do you think would happen across our country if, by design, there were a million of these kinds of meetings happening every month? This is just one example of an idea that can stir people's creativity and inspire an entrepreneurial revolution.

Chapter 9

Massive Leadership Impact...in One Year!

Here are some real numbers. There are 3141 counties, independent cities, and parishes across the USA. If we use simple numbers and divide the 50 million Americans currently on food stamps by 3141 counties, that means there are an average of 15,000 people on food stamps in EVERY SINGLE COUNTY in America.

While many of those people will want to stay in the bushel, I absolutely believe we can attract, encourage, inspire, and lead 2% of our fellow citizens to learn about the joys of entrepreneurship,

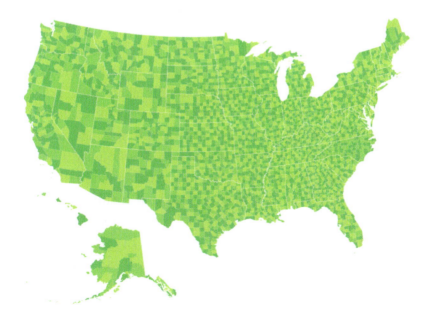

with no strings attached. These are motivated people who are willing and able to work hard. The key is they want to make a change in their lives.

That's 300 Americans. It will take servant leaders equipped with a BOLD attitude to share their storyline with Americans who have never heard the message of Small Business Freedom. After only one year using this simple math, we could encourage and exchange stories with 300 food stamp recipients in our local county. That means across 3141 counties, we could lead 942,300 Americans to take the first steps toward entrepreneurship. **That is nearly a million people!**

What do you think would begin to happen during that first year? Do you think those newly inspired apprentices of all ages are going to keep this to themselves? *Of course not.* Some will climb back into the bushel, but others would reach for their friends' hands. Local leaders could serve nearly 1 MILLION fellow Americans and inspire them to look outside of their current circumstances toward prosperity.

What if a few of the 300 folks got motivated, learned enough to take action, and created sufficient income to get off public assistance? Think of the stories they will tell. Some of our food stamp recipients would also get a different picture of entrepreneurs. It's reasonable to think some would gratefully apply their skills in part-time employment to serve one of our local, bold leaders.

Assuming we could quickly deliver this message to every county in the USA, it would not take long to encourage a million people to launch a cascade of new opportunities and tell others. Set aside for a minute the financial upside of creating new small business capital and reducing the public outlay for food stamps. Contemplate the impact on human capital. Even if 98% of the current recipients stayed on public assistance, our communities would benefit enormously.

What you might find uncomfortable in this simple illustration is the idea that business people would directly mentor food stamp recipients. You may be thinking that's not very practical. After all, food stamp people probably wouldn't want to learn about business. What does a food stamp recipient looks like in your mind's eye? Think back to the people we just discussed, like the college student, single parent, senior citizen, downsized, and underemployed worker.

Right now in America, according to U.S. Census data (http://www.census.gov/popclock/), there are over 315 million citizens. That means about one out of six people is on food stamps.

ONE OUT OF SIX!

Now look around your county again and ask yourself how many people you know who are silently praying to find a way back to economic self-sufficiency. On average, **one out of every six people you know** is on some kind of public assistance. These are our neighbors!

For some, this will become a way of life. America and her leaders have allowed this to happen, which in my view is an atrocity of epidemic proportions. We have allowed complacency to kill the American spirit. I realize there are also those in positions of power who have intentionally used public money and benefits to manipulate constituencies with freebies, but I am not going there right now. It is too easy to point the finger at politicos and blame them for all that ills us.

Right now, we will do more good by adjusting the mirror so we can see ourselves and ask these painful questions: *"How did I let this happen and what can I do to help fix it?"* You may be ready to start screaming at me because you believe you had nothing to do with this travesty. You have helped in your county. You support charities and donate your time. I understand your point. Please go with me down the rest of this road.

You may be the person looking for a way off food stamps or some other assistance programs.

You may be embarrassed that you had to apply for help in the first place. Don't be. We all have our stuff. Rest assured, nobody is going to ask if you are on food stamps. I know you are looking for a way to solve your own problem or you would not be engaged with me here. Believe it or not, there's an upside to where you are right now. Even though you may have a temporary financial challenge, when you get things turned around, you will be able to encourage someone else who is looking for a way to get out of the bushel.

This is about looking in the mirror and taking personal responsibility for our lives and helping others reject the victim mindset. Regardless of whether we are the mentor or the apprentice, together as citizens we need to man up and own the fact we are responsible for what America has become. Only then can we effectively take the next steps to rebuild the country. Something changes the moment you accept personal responsibility for your role in the nation's situation. Most importantly, you make it clear you intend to do something about it.

I use the 50 million food stamp example because it has been promoted in the media as a societal benchmark. My preference would be to celebrate the millions getting off food stamps, disability and other welfare programs and on to productive financial footing. In the next few sections, we will drill down into a number of specific plans PATRIOT MISSION has to create results for all the stakeholders in a local community.

When we as a Bold Leadership team take responsibility, we can lead our country to new heights!

Just to be crystal clear, I am **not saying** the enormous challenges we face today are because most business people intentionally threw Lady Liberty under the bus. Actually I would venture to say a vast majority of true blue U.S. small business people are proud of our heritage, thankful for the opportunity to live in a capitalist society, and have worked hard to build our enterprises. I am also not saying that having one meeting a month with folks who are struggling financially is going to solve the problems. That's just one example of how responsible leaders can craft solutions.

I am suggesting we will find answers much faster if we, as a leadership team, choose to accept ownership of the problems as well as the opportunities in America today. When we claim our stake in America personally, we show those who are watching what it means to be a citizen. It's not just about me. It's about us. When we model taking responsibility, whether we personally caused the problem or not, we are teaching those who are watching what leadership is all about.

Most people in America are not willing to take this position because most people are not leaders.

If America is to survive, it will only be because a team of passionate leaders pull out all the stops and, dare I suggest, ask for grace from the same God whom our Founders called on for "Divine Providence" as they wrote the Declaration of Independence.

What is a leader?

There are many ways to answer this question. Here's a simple definition.

DEFINITION: **Leader**—*noun*—A person who is in a formal or informal position to influence others[8].

I would like to share one of my favorite definitions. I first read this in a senior level leadership course when I was in college and it stuck with me ever since. Major C.A. was giving farewell instructions to the Graduating Student Officers of the Second Training Camp at Fort Sheridan, Wyoming, in 1917[2]. These officers were preparing to head into the difficult trench warfare and harsh conditions of the First World War.

As you read this brief excerpt of his remarks, think about our fellow citizens in the context of the soldiers. Put yourself in the role of the officer who is receiving instructions from Major Bach. The entire presentation is powerful. I have included a link and the full speech in the references.

Major Bach describes nine crucial leadership elements. I will share these and his perspective on moral ascendancy and self-sacrifice, which are especially relevant to our current discussion.

> "...You will ask yourselves: *"Of just what, then, does leadership consist? What must I do to become a leader? What are the attributes of leadership, and how can I cultivate them?"*

- Leadership is a composite of a number of qualities. Among the most important I would list self-confidence, moral ascendency, self-sacrifice, paternalism, fairness, initiative, decision, dignity, courage.

- Make light of your troubles, belittle your trials, and you will help vitally to build up within your organization an esprit whose value in time of stress cannot be measured.

- Moral force is the third element in gaining moral ascendancy. To exert moral force you must live clean, you must have sufficient brain power to see the right, and the will to do right.

- Be an example to your men. An officer can be a power for good or a power for evil. Don't preach to them—that will be worse than useless. Live the kind of life you would have them lead, and you will be surprised to see the number that will imitate you.

- A loud-mouthed, profane captain who is careless of his personal appearance will have a loud-mouthed, profane, dirty company. Remember what I tell you. Your company will be the reflection of yourself. If you have a rotten company it will be because you are a rotten captain.

- Great results are not achieved by cold, passive, unresponsive soldiers. They don't go very far and they stop as soon as they can. Leadership not only demands but receives the willing, unhesitating, unfaltering obedience and loyalty of other men; and a devotion that will cause them, when the time comes, to follow their uncrowned king to hell and back again if necessary.

- Self-sacrifice is essential to leadership. You will give, give all the time. You will give yourself physically, for the longest hours, the hardest work, and the greatest responsibility is the lot of the captain. He is the first man up in the morning and the last man in at night. He works while others sleep.

- You will give yourself mentally, in sympathy and appreciation for the troubles of men in your charge. This one's mother has died, and that one has lost all his savings in a bank failure. They may desire help, but more than anything else they desire sympathy.

- Don't make the mistake of turning such men down with the statement that you have troubles of your own, for every time that you do, you knock a stone out of the foundation of your house.

- Your men are your foundation, and your house leadership will tumble about your ears unless it rests securely upon them. Finally, you will give of your own slender financial resources. You will frequently spend your money to conserve the health and well-being of your men or to assist them when in trouble. Generally you get your money back. Very infrequently you must charge it to profit and loss."

Kind of gives you a different perspective, doesn't it?

Granted, we are not talking about leading a military organization, but if you understand America's survival is at stake, then I suggest we need to look at our roles as citizen leaders differently than we ever have. What if we took our roles as seriously as the Founders did theirs?

Let's take this discussion to another level and look through a different lens.

Public and private organizations that demonize free market capitalism are a big problem. These groups do not value our **7 LIBERTY Principles** and will not likely embrace the passion for America and the ideals edified by President Reagan or Major Bach. These groups relentlessly foster an over-reliance on government programs for long-term sustenance, like food stamps. They plant "dependency" seeds that have now grown into a massive weed field which choke the life out of the people who they claim to want to help. Their agenda is control not freedom.

Unfortunately, many good Americans have never been taught the true value of our free enterprise system. This is where bold leaders can make a difference. If we accept personal responsibility for allowing these falsehoods to dominate the local landscape, then our natural inclination is to do something about it.

Cleaning up the American landscape cannot be done in a weekend retreat or with a motivational speech. Replacing invasive, noxious weeds with healthy, organic seeds must happen consistently over time. We all know weeds can't simply be mowed down; they must be yanked out by the roots. The sooner we get busy pulling the weeds from the proverbial garden, the faster we will Rebuild America.

PLEASE HEAR ME. The weeds are NOT our fellow citizens. The weeds are the bad education, false teaching, and lies that have been propagated to keep people in bondage.

At first, starting this entrepreneurial revolution will be hard. Taking time to dig into this material is hard. Business is hard, the economy is hard, finding time and money to help others is hard. The weeds are thick and thorny. So what? When has anything worth fighting for been easy?

Put yourself in the socks of a citizen soldier on Christmas night, 1776. You are charged with crossing the Delaware River in the rain that will turn to sleet and snow as the darkness of night grips the partially frozen water. You march in silence with bloody, frozen socks (because your boots have worn out), and you have to surprise and beat the powerful Hessian soldiers at daybreak. The password for the night is "Victory or Death."

Now that my friends... was **hard**. And by the way, we won that battle... Merry Christmas!

A little history puts things in perspective, doesn't it? Relatively speaking, we have it easy. We get to lead a revolution while we build or support our local businesses and inspire people to live a better life.

How cool is that?

Chapter 10

Developing Strong Local Leaders

How do we begin to **BUILD** a Bold, Leadership team in every county?

We start by finding leaders who agree with this perspective and who are willing to make a decision to engage in this discussion. Some would-be-leaders may be squirming in their seats right now. "My plate is already so full; I cannot even imagine adding one more thing to it." I understand, but at this point I have not asked you to do anything. So relax and stay with me.

This is not a sprint. It is a very long ultra-marathon. The race will be won by taking one step at a time with our eyes glued to the Shining City trying to peek out over the horizon. When a small group of leaders each take one step, it can influence tens of thousands if not millions of people in a very short period of time.

Shortly, we'll dig into the details of exactly how we do this and what you can do to help.

We begin with leaders who can see past the dilapidated remnants of formerly great American cities. We need leaders who feel the pain and understand the travesty of Detroit, Michigan—the largest American city to declare bankruptcy. In counties that have escaped the tragedy of massive crime or economic collapse, entitlement pollution hangs in the air and chokes the local populous. Tough-minded patriots who remember what real productivity looked like in their local marketplaces will be relentless and undaunted as they build up people in their towns.

I'm sure many of our leaders will have never faced a challenge this significant. Most have probably never put their business venture into the mental framework of a combat engagement; but it most certainly is. We are at war with an ideology of apathy and surrender. When they look at us, our countrymen must see hope, optimism, and an absolute confidence in victory.

Imagine living in a community with a growing, strong, core leadership team who can be trusted to keep American values first. Consider the confidence inspired by a local team who can be depended upon to influence their marketplace with positive ideas and integrity. People who apply what they know to serve customers, inspire apprentices, and encourage startups.

This is how the energy of an entrepreneurial revolution begins to illuminate a city.

The ideal image you see in your mind's eye of the "Shining City on a Hill" is unique to you. The metaphor is something that every American can relate to, especially if we begin with a simple illustration like President Reagan gives us. The seed we plant and nurture in our mind becomes the driving motivation for us to step up and stay put until we win.

Imagine the impact when people from all walks of life, in every county, independent city, and parish across America decide to improve their own life and strengthen the foundation of their "Shining City." Of course the mental image is that of a city but it stands for the people. When people begin to experience true freedom and unlock their personal potential, they start to see themselves as a bright ray of optimism in their communities. That feeling will spread like wildfire… and people will come from miles around to watch it burn!

Developing Strong Local Leaders — 87

Where do we find these local leaders who will step up and play ball at this level?

We find these leaders in every single one of the 3141 United States Counties, Independent Cities, and Parishes. You know them personally. They go to your church, work with you, volunteer at the same service organizations, and support many of the same charities. As a matter of fact, since you are still going through this material with me, let's put your name on the volunteer list.

Here's the next challenge.

Zig Ziglar always used to talk about the most popular national radio station everyone listens to: **WIIFM**. Do you listen to it? Sure you do; "WIIFM = WHAT'S IN IT FOR ME."

I'm sure if you are a busy, entrepreneurial executive you may be starting to wonder how this can possibly work. You are extremely busy and while you are sympathetic to the challenges of those who are facing tough times, you just don't have time. Besides, this all seems a bit too idealistic.

"As a successful entrepreneur, the best I can do for America is to build my company, create profits, hire new people, pay my taxes, deliver great products or services, and vote during every election for candidates with whom I share common points of view." I agree, but let me ask you: have you ever heard the story of the goose that laid the golden eggs?

Here's what's in it for you. America is the goose and she's just about cooked. It is naive to think we can just bury our heads in the sand and somehow, somebody else will figure this out. You may have never considered this point of view before, but if you want to have any semblance of the free society we grew up with, then you have to step up and make a decision. YES or NO.

You have to choose. If you value the Shining City, you need to recognize you have been given much. If you are an American, you have been given a gift people around the world dream about. Imagine the boat people President Reagan talked about. They got into boats on the other side of the Pacific Ocean and set sail to get to America. Why? American Freedom.

> DEFINITION: **American Freedom**—*noun*—As stated in the U.S. Declaration of Independence, we define American Freedom as the unalienable rights of Life, Liberty, and the Pursuit of Happiness[9].

We must not ignore our responsibility to serve America while we build our businesses. A direct benefit for you is the opportunity to raise your game by joining a world-class team of players.

The PATRIOT MISSION Story will develop and promote a formidable group of leaders our adversaries will never see coming. We do not wield physical weapons or advocate violence. Those who do not share our point of view will not notice us at first because they don't value who we are or what we do. That is why I can offer this book and not be concerned about giving away the game plan. Obviously, I will not share all the details. Even if I did, if you have never built a business or passionately supported someone who has, this will sound like ideological mumbo jumbo.

As business leaders, we work in the trenches, with boldness, intensity, passion, and power to produce results. To execute our next step, which is to **GROW** our Capital, Political Influence, and Liberty, we must establish, inspire, and grow our bold leadership teams.

> DEFINITION: **Bold**—*adjective*—not hesitating or fearful in the face of actual or possible danger or rebuff; courageous and daring: a bold hero[10].

What is a **Bold** leader?

Simply put, the **Bold** leader is the first one on the team. She is the first one to throw her hat in the ring when there is a tough challenge. She does not care what others may think of her decision. He is the one who has enough personal experience to get in the fight because it is the right thing to do. He will leverage his confidence to recruit his own leadership team to get the job done.

Leaders from the President to the local pastor to the small business owner cast a vision for their people and teach new generations to do the same. Bold leaders are people who are willing to be vulnerable and admit they don't know everything. We must be strong enough to speak truth and call out excuses when we see them. In many cases, being bold is a learned skill and needs practice. In other cases, boldness may need to be tamed with humility.

We will begin to **BUILD** a **Bold** Leadership team with people across America for whom this message rings true. You don't need to be convinced, you just want to know what to do next. You have been looking for a team of like-minded patriots to join so you could do your part.

Next, we will train people to be **Bold**. There are plenty of good-spirited Americans out there, but in large measure they have been systematically gutted of their strength. Political correctness has weakened our country through fear tactics and intimidation. We will teach our team how to effectively overcome the tyranny of political correctness so we can reclaim our language and once again say what we mean and mean what we say. There is no boldness without backbone.

The Backbone of America cannot stand without **Bold** leaders in every corner of the nation!

Will you help us **BUILD** a Bold Leadership team in your county, city, or parish?

Chapter 11

Growing Critical Assets in 3 Steps

There is nothing more powerful on the face of this Earth than a principle-centered leader with a clear and compelling picture of the future in his mind. How do local, statewide, regional, and national leaders bring "The Shining City on a Hill" into focus? Recall President Reagan's description. "*... in my mind it was a tall, proud city built on rocks stronger than oceans, wind-swept, God-blessed, and teeming with people of all kinds living in harmony and peace; a city with free ports that hummed with commerce and creativity.*"

Notice the first part of this powerfully simple word picture. He describes what the city looks like. "*... a tall, proud city built on rocks stronger than oceans, wind-swept, God-blessed ...*" What must be in place for a city to stand tall and proud? She must have a rock solid foundation that can weather the constant pounding of the oceans and the prevailing winds.

For more than two centuries, America has weathered incredible internal and external storms because her people are strong and resilient. We have an amazing constitution that grants us the capability as a free people to decide our future. At this very moment in history we find ourselves at a crossroads. From my vantage point, if we are to remain and continually improve our role as an influential nation, we most **GROW** three key assets: Capital, Political Influence, and Liberty.

When we as individual citizens understand how these three resources impact our freedom and how we can exert direct control over each, then we can begin to rebuild America. The three are inexorably linked. Consider the synergistic power of educating and equipping a large number of people across America who step into a leading or support role in the small business environment. This leverage brings President Reagan's word picture to life: "*....teeming with people of all kinds living in harmony and peace; a city with free ports that hummed with commerce and creativity.*"

PATRIOT MISSION is a catalyst, built to connect the dots, create synergy, reduce wasted resources, and make full use of the small business talents, skills, insights, and support that already exist. We cannot take our eyes off the ball, because those who oppose our founding principles are relentless and undaunted in their pursuit to turn our view of a Shining City into a control zone where they decide what is best for us. This creates continued policies that yield poor education, more politics of division, and sustained class warfare. Despite attempts by many to subdivide the United States into classes or a hyphen society, we are not. We are Americans.

Leaders who espouse the **7 LIBERTY Principles** can rescue Detroit, Stockton, and countless other American cities facing the same peril if and only if we grow our capital, political influence, and liberty. We must do so quickly and in every corner of the United States. No doubt this is a tough road, but I submit explaining to our kids and grandkids that we caved in without fighting for them will be much harder. This entrepreneurial revolution will produce narratives that will be passed down to future generations. We have the opportunity to be the generation who decided to reclaim America, not let her ride off into the sunset as a broke, tyrannical, godless mess.

Some will argue it is not possible to have a simple discussion about growing capital, political influence, and liberty. The subjects are too broad and complex. They will say to suggest such an idea is to reveal my own naiveté. I beg to differ. I believe if we have anything but a simple conversation, we risk ending up back in the cesspool of theoretical grandstanding that is the hallmark of D.C. and many institutions of higher education.

The litmus test for me is whether we can implement, execute, and produce positive results in time measured in weeks, months, and years versus decades, centuries, and millennia. I know we can, because we already are. The 2020 Storyline paints the picture of where I believe we will be in the very near future. We will discuss the many ways YOU WIN by helping us get there faster.

Traditionally, entrepreneurs and small businesses operate in small, disassociated groups that rarely leverage their efforts consistently. **PATRIOT MISSION** is changing how American small business works, plays and lives together. The first step is to take the responsibility to GROW our personal and professional capital. As we do, this creates a supportive local structure this inspires individuals and companies. Next, we leverage our capital growth to influence policy which subsequently protects and expands liberty.

Our politicians have proven we cannot tax our way to prosperity (although it is hard to get that message by plugging into traditional information sources). We know all too well what happens when politicians waste our public capital, a.k.a. taxpayer money, and grow government unnecessarily. Liberty shrinks.

In his farewell address, President Reagan put it succinctly: *"As government expands, liberty contracts."* The corollary is also true. We know we can grow our way to prosperity and expand liberty, so let's talk about how we get there.

Step One: **GROW** our Capital, both personal and professional.

DEFINITION: **Capital**—*noun*—the wealth, whether in money or property, owned or employed in business by an individual, firm, corporation, etc. or an accumulated stock of such wealth[11].

Chapter 12

Step 1A—GROW Our Personal Capital

What is personal capital and why is it important to increase it?

For the purposes of this discussion, we will examine these three main components of personal capital: education, leadership, and money.

EDUCATION

Much is talked about education. We could engage in never ending debates about public education, vouchers, homeschooling, and school choice, but that is for another time.

In the context of capital, we want to focus on education that helps you produce results and improve your value in the marketplace. In my early business career after leaving the Air Force, as I drove from meeting to meeting, I constantly listened to cassette tapes. For the younger folks who don't know what those are, just ask your geezer parents.

I remember listening to a Jim Rohn audio cassette series called "Challenge to Succeed in the '90s." One of the quotes I remember clearly was: *"Formal education will make you a living; self-education will make you a fortune."* His point was clear. If we are going to succeed in business and in life, we are responsible for learning what we need to know. Many people confuse getting a good education with going to school and getting a piece of paper to hang on the wall. The two are very different.

Building personal education capital begins with a mindset around learning. You will find that people who are successful in any field are constantly learning. They are lifetime learners. You can discover how you learn best and select the formats most conducive to your learning style. You might prefer reading or listening to audio. Maybe you get the most out of video or tactile learning when you are actually doing something. Now with advanced technology, you can learn anytime and anywhere. Turn off the television and plug your ear buds into a mobile classroom.

Like so much of what we have already discussed, self-education begins with a decision to prioritize what you need to learn. A good place to start, if this concept is new to you, is to get a handle on your personal strengths. I recommend a book called *Strength Finders* 2.0 by Tom Rath. It's a short, easy read. At the end, you can go online and walk through an analysis that describes your unique strengths. By discovering where you are most skilled, you also learn about your blind spots.

A second book that can be very helpful is *One Big Thing* by Phil Cooke. Reading Phil's book will help you undercover your true passion and get clear on what you were born to accomplish during your time on Earth. Coupled with understanding your strengths, when you are absolutely certain what you are here to do, you can quickly accelerate your progress. Knowing these specifics about yourself is very helpful when you start working with mentors and building relationships to grow your businesses.

Your education should include continuous work on communication skill sets. How you share ideas both in the written and spoken word will make a world of difference in your success. Your appearance says a lot about you, too. You communicate confidence by the way you carry yourself. Speak well. Write well. Look sharp. Be sharp.

The most underrated communication skill is listening. As the adage goes, there is a reason God gave you two ears and one mouth. You always learn more when you ask good questions and listen intently to the response. Asking thoughtful questions also increases your conversational skills, which in turn can strengthen your relationship skills. Each of these has a cascading effect. Your decision to educate yourself and improve your skills will have lifetime benefits.

One of the most effective ways to rapidly grow your education capital and have a lot of fun is through personal experiences. Obviously, that happens every day as you live your life, but I am talking about something specific. When you plan an event or activity that is designed to give you an experiential education, you can rapidly accelerate your learning. This means changing your environment and getting out of your standard routine. This can happen when you meet new people, participate in conferences, and travel to new places to expand the horizons of your knowledge. Learning in this type of scenario can be a lot of fun, too!

In our time together, one of the themes I have hammered is the critical importance of understanding American history. While you can read and listen to books on endless historical topics, I suggest using the books as a primer followed by an experience to bring the subject to life. Travel to the places in the book. Get some perspective; feel what they felt.

How did the settlers travel?

Have you stood inside a replica of the Mayflower and wondered how in the world the Pilgrims actually made it across the Atlantic?

Read *Killer Angels; A Novel of the Civil War* and then walk the Gettysburg Battlefield with an expert guide. My family and I did. It's a powerful and moving experience. Go to Ford's Theater. Trace

John Wilkes Booth's getaway to the Surratt House then to Dr. Mudd's home where he got his broken leg splinted and finally to the rural Virginia barn where Booth met his demise.

Have you stood at ground zero in New York City, at the Pentagon or in the Pennsylvania Field? Ever wonder what it must have felt like to be attacked in the air or on the ground? Think about it.

America is less than 250 years old. When you travel internationally and study the roots of our ancestors, you can discover an entirely new perspective. Europe has a number of unique cultures and thousands of years of recorded history. Watch the movie *Monumental*. You will get an entirely new understanding of the guts, patience, and faith it took to leave Europe for Plymouth Rock.

In our **7 Founding LIBERTY Principles**, we refer to our Judeo-Christian principles. In the news, we constantly hear about the special relationship the U.S. enjoys with Israel. Why are the Jewish people and the Holy Land heritage so important to America? Regardless of your political or religious perspectives, the historical experience of traveling in the Middle East and specifically Israel can be life-changing.

These experiences, especially when guided by subject matter experts, can give you incredible insights, which will help you paint the "Shining City on a Hill" on the canvas of your mind.

When you passionately pursue self-education, learn your strengths, value other people in your communication, and personally experience America and key places around the globe, your personal capital grows immensely. The more education capital you possess, the more options you have. It does not matter whether you are 18 or 87. You have something to learn and to contribute. America needs your perspective.

LEADERSHIP

Whom do you prefer to follow—people who are well educated, good communicators, and have an experienced perspective? Me, too. I mentioned in the first Liberty Principle the adage, "Leader of one, leader of many. If you can't lead one, you can't lead any." With respect to personal capital, your decision to lead one, beginning with yourself, is paramount.

The truth is, if you have already taken responsibility for your education and acted on it, developing your personal leadership is a logical next step. You could argue this is simply another skill set, but I suggest it is much bigger than that. Leadership is where you begin to integrate personal core values into your daily work. It is where you demonstrate  to others by your actions what it looks like to be responsible and not a victim. This expands your education capital from a primarily inward focused activity toward an outward expression for others to see and experience.

As a leader of one, you will learn how to tell your story. You will realize how important it is to share your perspective. Stories are where we engage our fellow man. We may not always be right and if we develop good listening skills, we can learn where our viewpoints may be in error. Leaders learn to be humble, not arrogant. We learn to lead by serving others.

Leaders also need to learn why, when, and where to draw a line in the sand. Unfortunately in America, with political correctness infecting every level of society, many people are afraid to stand up and state clearly their position on a matter. Fear of offending someone frequently trumps standing for a principled position. A key skill leaders develop is the ability to fight for the ideas and beliefs that matter most to them. Not a physical fight, not even a loud boisterous fight, but a strong, well delivered argument defending a position of importance.

It takes practice to calmly articulate your position in a contentious situation. Especially when the other side uses tactics designed to inflame your sensibilities including name calling, outright lies, distortions, misdirection, extortion, and other emotion jarring negotiating tactics of the unprincipled attacker. Despite claims from many public officials for "civil discourse," we often experience anything but civility. How does a *leader of one* respond and carry the day?

First of all, by knowing where the line is and by being prepared. You must know what you believe and why you believe it. That's why we have clearly articulated specific founding principles. Knowing when to fight and when to come back and engage on your terms is a developed skill. Learning how to fight for what you believe with passion and strength while keeping your emotions in check is crucial. Unfortunately for many Americans, the issue is not the ability to fight. It is the fact they have no passion to fight for America. We must reverse this killer called apathy. We begin that process by growing our personal education and leadership capital.

MONEY

At the University of Maryland I majored in mathematics and minored in business. After taking many classes about numbers, including economics, accounting, and finance, I figured I knew what was necessary to run a business. After all, I was an experienced combat fighter pilot so how hard could it be to run a small business? That was the voice of ignorance. I had no idea what I didn't know. This is precisely the difference between book knowledge and real world experience. Until I started and ran my own company, I did not really understand business at all.

I am not alone. One of the biggest challenges we face in America today is financial literacy. That is the practical understanding of how money works in our homes, businesses, and in government. Effective marketers have done a fantastic job convincing Americans that delayed gratification is "old school" and we "deserve" the finer things of life now. Of course when you don't have the cash in the bank to buy those nice things, it means you have to borrow the money and pay interest.

It is hard to underestimate the importance of knowing how borrowing money for your first car or spending plastic credit to take a vacation you can't afford will impact your financial future. Since our country does not want anyone to feel bad because they don't have the money to buy the same car the neighbor bought or own a home, we have a big problem. The refrain "It's not fair" is commonly used to justify poor decision-making, especially financial choices.

Spending is out of control for many states and the federal government. America faces brutal choices that require financially literate people to make. Then citizens must be educated to understand and support these decisions. This is much easier said than done. Most citizens have no earthly understanding of how terrible our economic situation really is and what the future holds if we do not take massive action to change our position. Unfortunately, as we slide toward 50% of our population receiving some type of government assistance, there are a lot of truly ignorant people who do not understand the consequences of evading the hard decisions.

This is one reason why the PATRIOT MISSION is a generational fight. We must aggressively help three generations of

Americans get a grip on money. The number of people who do not know the basics should be cause for alarm. Getting smart on money matters is the key to becoming financially stable and strong. When your personal financial capital position is strong, it means you have not only knowledge but diversified assets and investment resources. When you have a basic understanding of the economy, you are a much more effective citizen.

The more **Personal Capital** you bring to the table, the more potential opportunity you have. You have direct control on how much personal education, leadership, and financial capital you can acquire. Once you set your personal capital growth plan on course, you can then begin to ramp up your **Professional Capital.**

Before we get into those details, I want to take a minute and go back to the mentoring opportunity we discussed earlier. Think back to the example we discussed where 100 local leaders invest 20 minutes a month with three people who want to change their lives. Imagine the impact of mentoring 300 people to substantially increase their personal capital in just one year. Even if only a few of those 300 people moved off public assistance and into entrepreneurial related activities for themselves or in the employ of others, how would that help your local county?

Now think about the nationwide impact of 300 people in each county; one million Americans taking responsibility for growing their personal education, leadership, and financial capital.

Just ponder that for a minute. We can do this.

Chapter 13

Step 1B—GROW Our Professional Capital

Professional capital is created by simply applying entrepreneurial strategies to personal capital.

Small business is an excellent training ground to help people develop professional capital. That means as we grow our personal education, leadership, and money, we can turn around and apply them to produce professional capital. In our discussion, we will examine three elements of professional capital including **intellectual property, teamwork, and small business**. Again, this is not an exhaustive list of capital categories, far from it, but it is a good place to start the discussion.

INTELLECTUAL PROPERTY

Most people don't realize they have ideas or knowledge that can be converted into cash. How many times in a week do you see a problem that could be solved by a minor tweak or a little creativity? What do you think the little patented paper sleeve around every coffee cup in America was worth? Someone actually thought of that, designed a prototype, filed a patent, sold the idea, and licensed the use of it to every major coffee franchise in the country.

Your ideas have value in the marketplace. You can create new products and services or make improvements to existing community favorites. How much value will depend upon many variables including the form your intellectual property takes, the channel through which you deliver the product, and the impact it makes on the end user.

As a way to understand the different options you have to develop your intellectual property, let's look at a simplified example. Suppose you are a healthcare professional with good scientific skills and a passion to help people with certain disease states.

You come up with a natural solution to a plaguing problem and you realize you can patent the unique formulation of ingredients. You could choose to pursue patent protection and classification as a drug. You know this will require years of human trials and millions of dollars of up-front costs necessary to comply with FDA regulations. When you formulate a drug, the long-term studies prove its function so you can claim a specific medical result.

Alternatively, you could choose to formulate your intellectual property as a nutritional supplement without the double blind, placebo controlled crossover trials and forgo the opportunity to make a drug claim. This option is a lot less expensive and a much faster path to market. However, you cannot make any drug claim that your supplement will heal, treat, cure, or ameliorate the disease problem. You can only educate the public and let them draw their own conclusion or you risk violating stringent FDA drug laws.

After an analysis of the potential market size, financial requirements, distribution channels, public perception of the problem, and receptivity to your solution, you get to decide what is best for you. Recognizing the value of your intellectual property is a key to success.

> DEFINITION: **Success**—*noun*—the favorable or prosperous termination of attempts or endeavors[12].

Maybe you are an avid social media user and you come up with an idea for a widget that makes something easier. You could translate the idea into an app prototype and then hire a programmer to build it. Once you test it and see if it works, just follow the protocols to protect your ideas and you might have the next blockbuster. Internet technology allows you to quickly ask people in a market segment if they care about your invention and, if so, how much they will pay for it.

Look around. There is no shortage of problems we can solve. Some ideas are practical and others are not. The point is as you build up your personal strengths, you cultivate your ideas. Your ideas and insights have potential in the marketplace when you believe they do. The difference in personal and professional capital is application. Many people simply do not believe their ideas are valuable so they do nothing to pursue their own intellectual property. What a waste.

The difference between you and others who are not plugged into a group like ours is confidence. You have discovered a safe place to develop your ideas. That's what PATRIOT MISSION is all about. We want to help you recognize the potential of your ideas. Developing your intellectual property is the first part of building your professional story and capital. Your rights to develop, own, and protect your ideas are guaranteed by the U.S. Constitution. Your ideas are your **personal property**, just like physical property. Now, let's discuss how to leverage your ideas through teamwork and business.

TEAMWORK

Teamwork is an overused word. Oftentimes it is used as a sweeping generality cast over large groups of people to inspire them to come together toward a goal. Frequently this is the case in sports, business, and in politics. Just because someone tells us we are on a team, doesn't mean teamwork will commence.

Have you ever been told you are part of a great team but did not feel like it at all? Unfortunately, many "Team Leaders" have positional authority but do not understand teamwork. This can be true of a boss who wants a company to work as a team even though he does not understand how to foster team spirit. You may have experienced a sports coach who was more concerned with his reputation rather than the players.

On the other hand, can you recall a time when you were part of a winning team? The difference between a team in name only and a world-class team boils down to fundamentals and execution.

This discussion will focus on **FIVE TEAMWORK FUNDAMENTALS** necessary for successful execution. These broad concepts only scratch the surface of the subject but establish a baseline for understanding as our teams begin to rebuild our nation.

1. The Benefits
2. The Qualifications
3. The Rules
4. The Impact
5. The Stakes

DEFINITION: **Teamwork**—*noun*—cooperative or coordinated effort on the part of a group of persons acting together as a team or in the interests of a common cause[13].

1. The BENEFITS

Why work on a team? Depending on your experience, you may or may not know the exhilaration of being a participating member of a world-class team. Many people are never encouraged in their lives, let alone invited to be part of a special, intimate group of professional teammates.

The first benefit you enjoy as part of a team is upgrading your skills. In a well-run team, whether it has 2 members or 50, you will improve far more than you will if you work by yourself.

> *"As iron sharpens iron, so one person sharpens another."*
> —PROVERBS 27:17

Developing teamwork skills is especially important for those who work alone (73% of the nearly 30 million small business owners are sole proprietors). Effectively working with other skilled people who have experience can have a big impact on your growth curve.

Good teamwork promotes continuous improvement of each member and the group at large. The mindset of each individual is crucial. Making the decision to improve in specific areas is the cornerstone to getting stronger as a team.

Mutual Support

I was fortunate to have been part of teams all my life. From a strong family team to sports teams to a combat fighter squadron; I have been blessed. The day I walked into undergraduate pilot training, I learned about mutual support; the importance of always knowing where your teammate is and watching his back. Depending on your relationship, mutual support can take on a number of different functions and is fundamental to success. The comfort and peace of knowing and trusting that someone truly has your back is an enormous benefit in great teams.

In the flying business we call this checking each other's six o'clock. It is very difficult to see an enemy aircraft or a surface-to-air missile when it is directly behind you. You have to be able to depend on your wingman to check your six and he depends on you for the same.

I still remember when I passed my final qualification check ride to become a Mission Ready F-15 pilot in the 27th Tactical Fighter Squadron. My commander, Lt. Col. "Bubba" Parker, encouraged me as the youngest "pup" in his squadron. Bubba told me I was joining a very elite group of people and that with my new leather jacket, my job was to be in position and watch my flight leader's six.

Good advice, Bubba. If you are a good leader and a strong teammate, your "young pups" will remember what you tell them for the rest of their lives. As the "pups" get sharper, you will see them begin to emulate the example you set. Continuous improvement and mutual support are burned into the fiber of our beings every time a strong team works together. Working together, you develop the kind of relationship that can be called on when everything is on the line.

Confidence

A challenge for many people in America today is combating fear. There are so many unknowns compounded by fear-mongering tactics from financial institutions, stressed out employers, government agencies, and the media. When you are by yourself, oftentimes you make the fear worse. What happens when you are in a place where you feel safe and productive? When you are working with people who are focused on growing stronger, supporting each other and winning, fear is replaced by confidence. As you become stronger, your confidence transfers to new players on the team.

Recognition—*Babies cry for it and men die for it.*

Recognition for strong performance is another teamwork benefit. When you set a goal, assign tasks, and hit the target on time and under budget, there should be a celebration. By effectively debriefing the team's activities, you can learn what went right and what could have gone better, all of which feeds continuous improvement. Recognition based on results is a logical extension of a positive team culture. Recognizing team members when warranted can create tremendous camaraderie and esprit de corps and serves to motivate others to do their best.

2. The QUALIFICATIONS

In my view, being trustworthy is the first qualification to join any team. I will paraphrase my recollection of the unique way Dr. Stephen Covey defined trustworthiness in his book *The 7 Habits of Highly Effective People*. He said you must have both character and competence to be worthy of trust in a particular role.

To be successful over the long term, you must be of sound character. In this context, this includes traits such as honesty, integrity, moral fiber, and strength of convictions. You develop your character over time with every decision you make and each action you take. The reputation you build over a lifetime will largely develop around your character. How do you treat people? Do you take responsibility for your mistakes or do you go into victim mode and blame others?

The second part of the equation is competence. You may have the character for a particular position, but if you are not experienced and skilled in the role for which the team is recruiting, then you are not qualified. Just because I have demonstrably strong character and a passion for football does not mean I am qualified to play offensive tackle for my beloved Washington Redskins. My high school football experience as an offensive tackle in the early

'80s does not quite meet the competence requirements to protect a professional quarterback in the pocket.

What is a good way to understand your competence?

Think about it this way. What can you contribute to a team? The easiest way to find out is to start with an inventory of your personal capital. This is why you need to catalog and be able to articulate your education, leadership experience, and financial resources, including tangible assets and knowledge. Then add your professional capital including intellectual property, teamwork, and business experience to round out your competence profile. Now you and the team leaders can objectively decide how you are best qualified to work with a specific group.

What are the qualifications you must possess in order to join a specific team?

Since teams are built for many different reasons, becoming a member may require all manner of skills and experience. Is this a personal or professional team? Depending on the nature of the team, you may or may not be qualified to join.

Here are a couple of basic examples.

If you are applying to join a business team or company, an objective presentation of your qualifications may take the form of a résumé. If you are looking to become an investor in a project, your qualifications may be limited to a financial statement. If you are considering starting your own team, you should qualify yourself based on the leadership and teamwork experience you have.

If you are trustworthy and want to join my team, the last qualification I require is that you be willing to play full out. This attribute is not skill dependent, it is attitude dependent. Teams with qualified people can get a task accomplished. World-class teams WIN BIG with passionate players who PLAY FULL OUT toward a powerful vision.

America needs trustworthy teams in every county playing FULL OUT to win our liberty back!

3. The RULES

What are the rules of good teams? Here are a couple of the basics to chew on.

Mission definition

An effective team must know specifically where it is going and why. Clearly stated goals, measured by time and objective benchmarks, are important. When the mission is clear, then the specific strategy and tactics can be broken down and assigned to the team members.

Qualified Leader

Teams must have a qualified leader otherwise they are a committee. The leaders are not necessarily the most senior people because effective teams should be run by those who are most competent in that arena. As an example, the great part about having digital natives in our midst is we (geezers) can follow our younger team leaders in areas where they have a distinct advantage. This can also be a great opportunity to mentor younger leaders in practical terms. While we geezers may not be social media geniuses, oftentimes we have other skills to contribute in marketing, management, and financial matters.

Followership

Being part of a team means knowing how to be a good leader AND a good follower—both are important. As a good team member, it is important to listen and learn when to share opinions and when to keep them to yourself. There is a delicate balance as you share your knowledge and experience while the younger leader is building her skill sets in front of the team. Humility in service to your team, regardless of experience, is important. Recognizing the contributions of others, regardless of their age, experience, and social status is crucial.

Standards

Let's say you have a big vision. Perhaps you want to rebuild a nation of 300 million people. You want to accomplish the vision in seven years, which requires involving people from all walks of life in every one of 3141 distinct geographic territories. To accomplish the mission, you will need to have tens of thousands of teams operating simultaneously.

Team Standards establish basic operating and administrative practices that each new member learns when they join the team. This enables team leaders to focus on key operational objectives rather than dealing with minutia. Shortly, we will discuss how monthly PATRIOT MISSION Leadership Development Programs will happen simultaneously in counties, independent cities, and parishes across America. Each of these events will be professionally facilitated with a turnkey operational system according to PATRIOT MISSION Standards.

When members join a local county chapter, they will be briefed on and expected to adhere to PATRIOT MISSION Standards during these programs. A standard can be as simple as turning off cell phones during presentations or maintaining confidentiality of private information discussed in a small group.

Standards raise the bar and establish levels of accountability that are clear and defined. Standards are explained at the beginning of team membership. All members need to understand and agree to them before moving forward. If a team member violates agreed upon standards, the leader is responsible to review the standards and determine if there is a misunderstanding or if the team member needs to be released.

Alligator Skin

Another important rule of effective teamwork is the need to put on your alligator skin. If you have never seen an alligator up close, just imagine how tough and thick their skin is. Your hide needs to be as tough as an alligator's. In the real world, not everyone gets trophies for just showing up. You must be able to handle and embrace constructive criticism.

The insane notion we can protect people from disappointment and that we ought to put self-esteem as the highest target of our focus without regard to performance is silly. It's been said feedback is the breakfast of champions. As individuals, we should seek out feedback on our performance so we can get better. The same is true of teams. If the leaders and members of teams do not foster a continuous improvement mindset, the value of teamwork quickly disappears and the potential for capital growth dies with it.

4. The IMPACT

The impact of focused, mission-specific teamwork is tremendous. Fortunately, teamwork skills translate to your personal and family life, small business development, and national restoration.

While entrepreneurs tend to be rugged individualists at heart, there is a way to leverage teamwork to serve both our personal businesses and the community at large. It depends on how you see things. If you have to be "the man" in all cases and you need to come up with all the ideas, make all the decisions and keep all the money, then it's likely you will not be interested in teamwork.

If you are one of the 22 million sole proprietors in America, this teamwork discussion may be challenging. Old philosophy would suggest you need to keep everything to yourself and build a wall around your enterprise. While it's certainly important to protect your intellectual property, you must realize that you can leverage your skill sets by working with others who complement you. Build a strong team of dependable players and ask how you can best support them.

A friend of mine recently told me of a discussion he had while on an international trip. He was on a private historical tour and met a man who was in the top echelons of Major League Baseball management. The executive explained many people think baseball is a team sport, but really it is a group of talented individuals performing on a field with each other to win a game. The athletes need the team to showcase and monetize their talents. The team needs the athletes to make up the roster and draw the crowd. It's a symbiotic relationship and similar to the local small business environment.

If you own a company, building strong inside teams can transform your business. It will challenge you to grow your personal leadership skills. Using effective teamwork can unlock creativity and build an atmosphere of trust and accountability like nothing else can. You can upgrade your culture so new leaders emerge in your midst who embrace the opportunity to grow their personal capital which directly impacts their work productivity and your bottom line.

Teamwork is essential to grow our professional capital. When we model it, practice it and nurture it, we reinforce the value of strong teamwork.

5. The STAKES

What makes the difference between winning and losing when everything is on the line?

It's certainly not experts' opinions. I contend it is not necessarily having the best and brightest people on the team, but rather having a fired-up, focused group who is absolutely sold out to the mission. They are hungry and can taste victory. The team has practiced, role-played, tested strategies, and mentally prepared as if everything is on the line... because it is.

What does winning mean to you?

Step 1B—GROW Our Professional Capital — 115

Political correctness disease has permeated teamwork primarily because non-performers and partisans have tried to make winning a zero sum game. Their weak argument is when we win someone else has to lose. In combat, that's a good idea. If we commit troops to any war zone, there should be a clear point of demarcation that indicates when we have won the fight.

However, small business is not a zero sum game. We live in an era where technology, teamwork, a passion for mentoring a new generation, and other liberty-based motivations open up new worlds to entrepreneurs. It's time to think differently about how we can WIN together. Every teamwork experience you have compounds your professional capital.

PATRIOT MISSION will set a new standard for entrepreneurial teamwork. Between now and the completion of our 2020 Storyline, we will inspire tens of thousands of small business teams to create products, services, relationships, and experiences we can't even imagine right now.

In many cases, you won't realize how valuable your teamwork experience is until you get to play in a high stakes game. I had no way to know less than two years after I passed my check ride with Bubba, our team of fighter pilots, maintainers, and support personnel would launch our first Desert Storm combat sorties. As I walked out of our makeshift operations bunker, I glanced up at a six-foot sign we brought with us from our home squadron in Virginia. The sign simply read: "LEAD, FOLLOW OR GET THE HELL OUT OF THE WAY." I knew I was on a world-class team ready to FLY, FIGHT and WIN... and we did!

Here's an American high stakes teamwork flashback that will bring a smile to your face.

I remember a very cold Friday night in February of my junior year in high school. A bunch of my classmates and I got together at our buddy Don's house in Bowie, Maryland to watch a hockey game. It was not just an ordinary game; this was the matchup that would determine who would play for the Olympic Gold Medal in the 1980 Olympics. The matchup:

The United States of America versus The Union of Soviet Socialist Republics (USSR)

The experts gave the USA team zero chance of beating the Soviets because we had not done so since 1960. It's also important to remember at the time, the Olympics were supposed to be for amateur athletes, but the Communist countries trained their players as professionals from the time they were very young children.

In 1980, we were at the height of the Cold War with the USSR. The Berlin Wall was still standing. We were in miserable economic conditions, our hostages were being held in Iran and there seemed to be nothing but malaise in America at the time... until Friday night, February 22nd, 1980.

Despite all odds after being behind 3—2 going into the third period, the U.S. upset the Russians 4–3 and went on to win the Gold Medal after beating Finland. Sports Illustrated named the "Miracle on Ice" the Top Sports Moment of the 20th Century. If you have never seen the 2004 movie, MIRACLE, I'd suggest you do. It will fire you up.

What are the stakes in America right now?

Ladies and gentlemen... everything is on the line in America today. Faith in government institutions is at an all-time low. We have to rebuild trust at the grassroots level, county-by-county. Principle centered teamwork and strong leadership are the cornerstones necessary to successfully execute the entrepreneurial revolution and turn our nation around. The great part about building entrepreneurial teams is everyone who believes they can contribute and wants to play full out can help us WIN.

Let's look at how we merge our intellectual property and teamwork into business models to launch our professional capital growth plan.

Small Business

The actual business venture is the result of your focused attention on your personal and professional capital. It is the public representation of who you are as an entrepreneur. A small business is a direct expression of our pursuit of happiness. It is the tangible entity to which we have been guaranteed personal property rights by our Constitution.

The income, profit, and equity you enjoy as the owner of your venture are the financial benefits for which you have worked long and hard. The return on your investment of time, financial capital, and other resources will be measured by the market. Sometimes that's great, other times it's not so much fun.

As Michael Gerber says, "The purpose of a business is to sell it." Even if you never considered selling 'Your Baby,' Michael points out, if you don't sell it to a third party that means you are buying it yourself; make sure it is worth the price you are paying. Businesses are designed to create financial value and need to be measured as such. When you develop your intellectual property and effectively use teamwork, your firm can test and employ creative business models and substantially grow in value. Then you have options. You can keep the company, sell it and start a new one, or cash out. Perhaps then you may choose to become an angel investor and mentor a new generation of entrepreneurs.

Growing our business capital has a major impact on our county, city, or parish. Expanding companies create jobs, increase the tax base, provide products and services to consumers and enhance the community's image to other businesses looking for a good place to relocate. Some will create multiple county, state, regional or national locations. Grassroots synergy develops when entrepreneurial companies are systematically inspired, spawned, grown, and eventually sold or passed down to a new generation. Confidence grows in the local market because it means your county is a good place to start a business, get a job, and learn about entrepreneurship.

When this is done well, the community and its leaders get the credit. Who are the leaders that make this work? Everyone who commits to **GROW** their personal and professional capital has a stake in the success and can be recognized as such. Most importantly, the result is not a one-time good deal. It is a systematic method to grow our capital in any county, city, or parish where there are at least three people who are ready to go to work. Some might call it an execution model for an entrepreneurial revolution. There's an idea.

> *"A person standing alone can be attacked and defeated, but two can stand back-to-back and conquer. Three are even better, for a triple-braided cord is not easily broken."*
> —Ecclesiastes 4:12

Chapter 14

Step 2—GROW our Political Influence

Why is it important to grow our political influence?

It's been said that all politics are local. However, many people I have spoken with during the last several years have virtually no idea what is really happening in local politics nor do they much care. This is especially true for people who are under significant financial stress. The people who are most plugged into political matters seem to be profitable business owners who are active in the community as well as citizens who follow politics.

Political Science is called science for a reason. There are multiple variables that impact elections and the success or failure of a particular candidate or ballot initiative. During election season, the majority of the money and therefore attention is driven to national and to a lesser degree, state or local contests. At the end of a long campaign season, especially in years when we elect a new President, most people are completely fed-up and don't want to think about politics for the next year or two. That is certainly understandable and I share the frustration. Here's the challenge, though. The people and issues for which we cast ballots determine so much about our future.

Sadly, an enormous number of citizens do not even value their constitutional right enough to go to the polls and cast a ballot. Most citizens do not comprehend the complex decisions and resulting power elected officials have to influence their lives.

Again, this topic qualifies for several libraries of books, videos, newspapers, historical analysis, and certainly field trips, which are all beyond the scope of the course now. What is within the scope is to share why we are including political influence as a topic in a business discussion, where we draw the lines, and how we expect to encourage people to participate politically.

Even though I've said it before, just for the record let me reiterate that PATRIOT MISSION is a for-profit business, not a political organization. As a business organization we DO NOT promote candidates, political issues or ballot initiatives. WE DO strongly advocate to anyone who will listen to our unwavering position that every single citizen should engage in the political process. At a minimum we encourage people to get to know local politicians, study the issues, learn how to ask hard questions, and understand the impact of the policy positions they take.

One of the main reasons America is facing extraordinarily difficult circumstances now is because the vast majority of citizens do not understand what politicians on both sides of the aisle have done and are doing to impact our liberty. Here's a simple exercise. Ask 10 people about their Social Security account. You may be shocked to find out how many people actually think the money deducted from their weekly paychecks is going into a fund with their name on it that earns interest.

They mistakenly believe when they hit retirement age, the good stewards at the U.S. Department of Treasury simply return their principal and interest as a monthly stipend from the account they have paid into for most of their lives. Sorry, Charlie. Your money was spent long ago. We have to increase taxes as well as borrow money from your kids and China to make good on payments due to you.

We experience the impact of political influence every day of our lives. Laws are created by the legislative branches of our state and federal governments and signed by their chief executive; either a governor or president. These politicians make decisions based on the influence of those who elect them. Politicians are also influenced by their personal ideologies, lobbyists, the customs of the legislative bodies in which they serve, and the media's portrayal of their positions.

If we look at government performance through the lens of small business, we can keep things simple. Look at results, key metrics, financial statements, and satisfaction of the stakeholders. Across the board, most people agree with the hard data. We have a skyrocketing national debt, growing budget deficits, no operating budget, swelling welfare programs, and an unserviceable amount of unfunded liabilities. In business terms, we call that bankrupt.

How did we get here? Who made the decisions that have allowed America to get in this position? Didn't anyone see this coming? What can I do to influence change? I'm only one person.

This is the challenge AND the opportunity. These are fair questions, but at the end of the day, while we must analyze and debate the root causes of the problem, we must focus on influencing corrective action. Some will argue we have already driven over the fiscal cliff and there is nothing we can do. I disagree.

Many Americans are under the false impression we live in a democracy, which in simple terms is "mob rule." Our Founders designed America to be a Representative Republic to ensure we would have equal representation no matter where we lived or who we were. Citizens need to understand these political fundamentals in order to realize they can make a difference.

While we certainly do not have any time to waste, I believe we can rapidly influence change if we are decisive, stay moored to the Constitution, and work together as a smart team. The fastest way to elicit change is to shift the way people see things, which is called a paradigm. Let me suggest an old versus new political paradigm.

OLD Political Paradigm	NEW Political Paradigm
1. Business and politics do not mix.	1. Business and politics are ALREADY mixed.
2. My vote does not matter.	2. Every vote matters.
3. Political correctness rules the system.	3. Leverage can change a broken, politically correct system.
4. Let lobbyists and parties pick the candidates.	4. Develop grassroots candidates with common beliefs and promote them to the parties
5. Politicians do not listen to "WE THE PEOPLE."	5. If we manage our employees well, they produce agreed upon results or they get fired.

NEW Political Paradigm

1. Business AND politics are already mixed.

We need to reset our thinking from business OR politics to business AND politics. The money we produce from our companies is the fuel that drives politics. Business people are the key to politics. The only question is whether business people are ethical and play by the rules. How many become crony capitalists and get in bed with the government and play two sides against the middle?

We may not choose to make our political views a part of our interaction with employees and/or customers. However, we must make our views known to those whom we hire to represent us. Government financed decisions including taxation and spending issues are made on a local, state, and federal level. They have enormous consequences on the health and vitality of our nation's economy. Business people are the best equipped citizens to ask tough questions and stave off non-answers.

2. Every vote matters.

Every election cycle, we hear about races that are decided by a handful of votes. When you consider only about half the eligible voters cast a ballot in the U.S., if even a small percentage of voters believed their ballot mattered, we would see a significant difference in turnout.

Let's use averages and round numbers. There are approximately 30 million small businesses in the U.S. Since business people are generally more plugged into political matters, let's be generous and say that 65% cast a ballot. That means that 35% or 10,000,000 small business owners do not vote. If half of these non-voters believed their votes counted, then 5,000,000 more votes would be cast. (FYI, the difference in the 2012 Presidential popular vote was less than 5,000,000 votes.)

3. Leverage can change a broken, politically correct system.

What creates legitimate political leverage? The answer is the powerful influence of a large, well informed, engaged, and fearless electorate. Citizens who understand "The Shining City on a Hill" know political correctness is a terminal disease. If a handful of rich donors and insiders think they can get away with doing deals in smoke-filled rooms while using political correctness to keep the uniformed in check, they will. Crooked politicians run scared when they have no place to hide. Like in any fight, if you have leverage, use it. WE THE PEOPLE create major leverage.

People who used to believe politically correct positions and voted blindly along party lines will wake up. They will become informed by their personal experience as opposed to believing what they hear in a speech. This makes politicians very nervous. Take for instance 10 or 20 million young people who figure out the government has robbed them of their future, killed the economy, and stuck them with the tab. As a team, WE THE PEOPLE wield the political influence and leverage to change a broken system.

4. Develop grassroots candidates with common beliefs and promote them to the parties.

Over time, our local leadership development programs will spawn potential candidates who will be interested in serving. As opposed to career politicians, they will be in position to give back to the community as citizen politicians for a period and then return home. They will be strong leaders who have built successful businesses. Some, not all, will consider running for elective office if asked, especially if they are plugged into a strong and vibrant support system that is engaged in the political process.

Other leaders may serve in political party activities or quietly behind the scenes in ways more suited to their skills and passions. Perhaps they will volunteer to make phone calls, host formal or informal forums. The key word is serve. People who answer the call to serve with an expectant attitude of success make good things happen.

5. If we manage our employees well, they produce agreed upon results or they get fired.

Politicians are employees. They make a sales pitch, a.k.a. campaign. When the majority of the electorate buy their pitch, the politician is hired for the new job and goes to work. WE THE PEOPLE hire them based on their campaign platform and the promises they make. We pay them with our tax dollars to represent our best interests. If they run for reelection, we measure their performance against previous promises delivered.

Would you hire an employee and then check in a year, two, three, four, or five years later to see how they are doing? What are the odds they would stay on track? **About Zero.** Could you legitimately expect them to be accountable if you never did a performance review? Of course not. When citizens make the mental shift to understand elected public employees are working for them, paid by tax dollars withheld from their paychecks, then we can begin to drive accountability.

While many politicians have honorable intentions when they take office, without strong accountability, it is easy to get off track. Just like market forces, there are tremendous political forces that will do their best to shape the actions of our elected officials. Many of these forces are diametrically opposed to the **7 LIBERTY Principles.** This means we must, as a citizenry, stay vigilant and actively involved so our elected officials do not get too far off the reservation. As the leaders of their businesses, owners and engaged employees should set the pace for civic participation in their communities.

PATRIOT MISSION encourages every citizen to engage in the political process. We should have spirited debates among ourselves to understand the issues and the consequences of decisions. As citizens, we can plug into grassroots political organizations that represent our perspective and learn from them. We can contribute our time and effort to support groups who serve similar objectives. Go to events, attend forums, see what happens in your local community, and express your opinion.

We must develop critical thinking and analytical skills to navigate beyond political spin and drill down into the real results. When we do, candidates, elected officials, and supporters of specific ballot initiatives will feel the political influence of an informed electorate. They will also begin to develop a renewed, healthy respect for WE THE PEOPLE.

As a small business community, we must be engaged ALL THE TIME, not just in election season.

The challenge is unless we have a simple plan that seamlessly integrates political discourse and accountability into our everyday business activity, then politics will be viewed as an outside distraction. When we talk about *The **MADE IN THE USA Project**™*, you will see how we built a fun program that incorporates this type of involvement without being onerous or boring. When people move from the old to the new political paradigm, we can influence a seismic shift in the political landscape.

Helping people **GROW** their personal capital is a great segue into learning about capitalism and building professional capital. Once they become competent and confident developing their professional capital, then it is possible to have a direct influence on local, state, and national politics. When millions of Americans individually express their political influence at the ballot box, then we can defend our Liberty. When we raise our game a few notches, we will boldly take back lost territory and actually **GROW** our Liberty.

Chapter 15

Step 3—GROW Our Liberty

Taken by itself, the idea of growing liberty may seem abstract. When you understand the first two steps of growing our capital and political influence, then growing liberty is easier to see. It is the natural result of steps one and two. In order to preserve our liberties for future generations, it is absolutely crucial we understand how these dots connect. Otherwise, we will be passengers on the good ship America floating aimlessly on an open ocean.

> DEFINITION: **Liberty**—*noun*—freedom from arbitrary or despotic government or control[14].

By definition, if we want to grow liberty, then we must continually grow our freedom from government control. When in your lifetime have you seen the government's appetite for control shrink? Correct answer… NEVER! We must encourage our elected politicians to honor their promises and represent their constituents. Elected officials must believe a strong, educated electorate will hold them accountable. They need to hear the voice of sweet reason reverberating in the back of their minds: "*Represent us as you promised or you will be fired when your contract comes up for renewal!*"

Even in rare instances when those in authority work to reduce government's size, influence, and control, their comrades in the legislative chambers are fighting to increase the power of local, state, and federal governments. In simple terms, growing government equals bureaucratic control. Reducing government (not just reducing the rate of growth) means WE THE PEOPLE get more control.

Liberty... USE IT OR LOSE IT.

Liberty is like physical fitness. If you want to be in top condition, you can't go to the gym once a year, say on July 4th before the cookout, and expect to maintain peak performance. Liberty is the same. If we don't stay vigilant, like a creeping muffin top, one day we will wake up and discover we are FAT and controlled by an elitist government who tell us what to eat and when.

Liberty requires recognizing the unsung heroes who are called to serve in ways we cannot understand. We must Honor those who physically protect liberty. Think of those who protect liberty at its most basic level... LIFE. Think of emergency personnel who come to our rescue, running up the stairs into burning buildings and sprinting toward exploding vehicles. Medical teams save our lives and deliver God's miracles on a daily basis. We grow our liberty by speaking out to support those who selflessly put their lives on the line for us.

I've said repeatedly our entrepreneurial revolution is not violent. But our military and law enforcement agencies are in a dangerous, armed fight every single day. They wear weapons because people who HATE AMERICA are on a mission to kill them (and us). Our adversaries hate us because of the God-fearing principles upon which our country is founded. You cannot reason with or rehabilitate evil. You must eliminate it. I realize some contend if we are more polite and less exceptional, the haters would like us more. **Nonsense.** Just ask the terrorists. They are happy to explain why they hate us and will not stop until we either see it their way or die. Cut and dried. So to our heroes who bravely guard our Liberty in faraway places and at home: **THANK YOU.**

Liberty requires us to defend our religious freedoms. As I mentioned earlier, the Founders made it crystal clear in the Declaration of Independence that "Divine Providence" is the source of Liberty. Let's reach back and see what our third President had to say about it. Next time you are in Washington, D.C., go to the Jefferson Memorial, look up and read the Rotunda Inscription.

"I have sworn upon the altar of God eternal hostility against every form of tyranny over the mind of man."
—Excerpted from a letter to Dr. Benjamin Rush, September 23, 1800

DEFINITION: **Tyranny**—*noun*—arbitrary or unrestrained exercise of power; despotic abuse of authority[15].

That looks to me like the exact opposite of liberty. I believe it is reasonable to assume President Jefferson swore eternal hostility against anything that would take away our liberty. I concur.

This brings us back to the tough part of the message. WE THE PEOPLE must take responsibility for preserving, protecting, and growing our liberty. We must teach, friends, family, colleagues, and our next generation what Liberty is, why it matters, and how to **GROW** it.

Benjamin Franklin put it well when he said: *"They who can give up essential liberty to obtain a little temporary safety, deserve neither liberty nor safety."*

- Freedom is hard.
- Defending Liberty is hard.
- Crossing the Delaware and scaling the cliffs at Normandy were hard.
- Taking Hamburger Hill was hard.
- Honoring the oath of office by resisting excruciating torture at the Hanoi Hilton was hard.
- Marching and going to jail to demand civil rights was hard.
- Flying to the moon, landing, and returning men safely to Earth was hard.
- Climbing up the stairs into the burning World Trade Center buildings was hard.
- Running toward the explosions in Boston was hard.
- Looking for terror cells house to house and avoiding roadside bombs is hard.
- Taking financial risk, hiring employees, and building a small business is hard.

It is hard to GROW our Capital, Political Influence and Liberty.

So what?

If you want easy, hop on the exit ramp out of America; it's wide open. You have a choice: fight for what you believe or roll over and quit. There is no middle ground. An answer of maybe is the same as quitting. If you are not sure what you believe, revisit our **7 LIBERTY Principles**. See how those strike you.

As for me and my house, we will serve the Lord and fight for freedom in America.

Together we are writing a new chapter in America's story. Many people thought **The PATRIOT MISSION Story** was only about rebuilding America's economy through entrepreneurship. Small business also has the power to illuminate the magnificence of America and to teach a new generation how amazing our nation is. As we GROW our Capital, Political Influence and Liberty in this new paradigm, we will be planting the seeds to inspire men and women who are not even alive yet to stand strong, protect Lady Liberty, and change the world! I hope you will join us.

PART III

WHAT IS THE ACTION PLAN TO REBUILD AMERICA?

"The best way to predict the future is to create it."

— Peter Drucker —

Chapter 16

Planning the Mission

Let's connect the dots and pull **The PATRIOT MISSION Story** together.

A while back I mentioned ours is a David versus Goliath story. Think about the fledgling leadership team in your county as David's team. In order to take on the "Goliaths" of entitlement syndrome, apathy, and economic malfeasance, we need to bring together the key elements of our game plan so they can be executed and the storyline can be fully developed.

Since Goliath doesn't represent a particular individual or group of people, we don't need an armed revolution or a slingshot to defeat him. What we need is a new line of thinking; a new way to understand how people can reach their goals, dreams, and aspirations. We need the toughness to stand up and fight for what we believe. We need the resolve to step up and take action.

Let me map out how we beat Goliath using an example from my flying days.

In planning combat missions, the flight lead is responsible to map out fundamentally sound strategies and tactics to accomplish the goals for that day. He is assigned a specific mission objective, provided dedicated resources, and must prepare a plan to be on target on time. The flight lead briefs the mission to the team members and support crew. This includes launch timing, targets, threats, and benchmarks necessary to complete the mission successfully.

At the end of the day, mission success depends on execution. You can have a phenomenal plan on paper, but if you don't execute it well, you lose. In the case of combat missions, poor execution means we miss the target or worse yet, a comrade in the air or on the ground is killed in action. None of the above is acceptable. We have a saying in the Air Force: *"Flexibility is the Key to Airpower."* Why? Missions do not always go as planned.

This is why strong leadership is so important to mission success. Leaders who are grounded in core principles, well trained in operational standards, and mentored by experienced instructors make good decisions in the heat of battle. Those who are weak on fundamentals cannot be trusted in the most harrowing of times. You really find out what someone is made of when the shooting starts. When leaders make bad decisions, the consequences can be catastrophic. During Desert Storm, I was privileged to serve with a number of outstanding leaders.

The same rules apply to building a business and working to save a nation.

We need a clear target, strong leadership, and specific goals. **LEAD. BUILD. GROW.** We also need to be flexible and keep our heads on a swivel so we can see what's going on around us. Check six.

As we move forward, I will describe in detail the systems and strategies through which PATRIOT MISSION is bringing our Dream, Vision, Purpose, and Mission into reality, county-by-county. Before we make the transition from strategic to tactical execution, I want to take a few moments and pull back the curtain so you can see how **The PATRIOT MISSION Story** came to life. I hope my experience will encourage you to find a mentor and submit to his leadership.

Hopefully you enjoyed Michael Gerber's remarks at the beginning of our story. If you didn't read the foreword, I would encourage you to do so. What I am going to share with you is how Michael came into my life as a mentor, leader, friend, and ardent supporter of PATRIOT MISSION.

One of the habits I developed as a young man was to keep a recommended list of good books to read. I kept a list in an old calendar portfolio I started using in college. When the Air Force made the transition to Total Quality Management, I read Stephen Covey's *7 Habits of Highly Effective People,* and it revolutionized my way of thinking. I upgraded my calendar and started mapping out my life in terms of roles and goals. My reading list then took up residence in my new 7 Habits Planner® so I could balance my reading among the key roles in my life.

In 1996, someone recommended I read a book called *The E-Myth*. I dutifully placed it on my reading list among the other 30 or so books to be read at the time. I'm sorry to say I did not stop what I was doing and read it then. Had I done so, I am sure it would have saved me a decade or more in hard lessons. Fast forward to the summer of 2000, when I was delivering a keynote address to an audience of about 1000 people in Canada. The topic had to do with raising standards in business.

After my presentation, I was visiting with well-wishers who were thanking me for the speech. One lady in particular asked me a poignant question. *"The subject you covered is similar to what I read in Michael Gerber's book. Have you ever read The E-Myth?"* I smiled politely and responded that in fact the book was on my list, but I had yet to read it. After I left the meeting, I didn't give the *E-Myth* another thought.

I distinctly remember flying back to Florida on a Friday afternoon. I returned home to my bride and two young girls, who were nine and seven at the time. Nancy had a busy week while I was on the road, so I gladly offered to take the girls out and wander around for a few hours.

Our first stop was a local bookstore in the Indian River County Mall. This is a great place to hang out because the girls could go to the kids' section and read their books, draw pictures, and play games. While they were enjoying their entertainment, I wandered into the business section which was right next to the kids. The bookstore marketers were smart. I could keep an eye on my girls and peruse the interesting business titles at the same time. As I turned to look at the shelves, there was a book that seemed to fall off the shelf. It hit me exactly at eye level and you probably already guessed… it was *The E-Myth Revisited*. (I had procrastinated so long, Michael already published an updated version!)

Well, I may be thick, but I didn't need any more signs to tell me I should read this book. I might add, if you have not read it do not wait another minute (after you finish this book, of course.) I bought my copy and gathered the girls for some food court delights, a lap around the mall, and a return trip home. By the time we got back to the house, I had already read the introduction, both covers, and a few tidbits inside.

What followed was the single most joyous and frustrating weekend of my entire life. I remember sitting in my office reading the book from cover to cover. I was so mad at Mr. Gerber because I could not figure out how he could tell my story of entrepreneurial chaos so well and not pay me a royalty. Several times I threw the book across the room. Nancy was sure I had lost my mind.

Michael is a true legend in entrepreneurship, having helped transform 70,000-plus businesses in 145 countries over the past 25 years. *The E-Myth Revisited* has sold over 5 million copies around the world, is a New York Times Bestseller, and has been used as a textbook in dozens of different languages in universities around the world. Michael says his ability, insight, and understanding about entrepreneurship is truly a gift from God. I am thankful to have been a direct beneficiary.

Through a series of circumstances that can only be described as miraculous, my team and I met Michael for the first time in Seattle on Labor Day Weekend, 2000. In the years that followed, I have enjoyed a personal relationship that has challenged me at many levels. In 2005, Michael invited me to come to work with him for a number of years on a new business. During our time together, Michael developed an intensive he calls *In the Dreaming Room®*, where he personally led hundreds of people to capture their most passionate entrepreneurial dream.

This brings me back to **The PATRIOT MISSION Story**. Because of my work with Michael, I was blessed to go *In the Dreaming Room®* more than a dozen times. Over a period of years, this is how the PATRIOT MISSION came to be from a blank piece of paper. Here's how Michael describes his strategy to "*Awaken the Entrepreneur Within®.*"

> "So, you want to be an entrepreneur, but you just weren't born with that skill? Nonsense! Anyone can learn how to be an entrepreneur.
>
> The problem is that everybody believes entrepreneurs are born, not made. Well, I know that entrepreneurs are not those few gifted geniuses like Steve Jobs, or Bill Gates, or Anita Roddick, they are in every single one of us. But, because nobody thinks like that, few of us ever are taught how to awaken that entrepreneur that lives within each and every one of us.
>
> In order to get in touch with your inner entrepreneur, you must start with a blank piece of paper and beginner's mind. Then, you must let yourself dream. What do you see for yourself and your business in the future?

If you can define these four things, you can build a thriving business:

Dream   The end game, or the great result. The higher aim. Why does the world need your business? *(My Dream is to transform the state of entrepreneurship and small business worldwide.)*

Vision   The mechanism through which the Dream will be realized. The Vision shows you how to achieve the Dream. *(My Vision is to invent the McDonalds of small business development services.*

Purpose   Ask yourself, "why" and "for whom" am I building this business? Your intention. *(My Purpose is to transform the lives of new entrepreneurs and small business owners.)*

Mission   The task at hand. The actions that need to be carried out. The Mission brings the Dream, Vision & Purpose into reality. *(My Mission is to create the turnkey system through which emerging companies will grow, prosper, and flourish, to be delivered at less than the cost of a minimum wage employee, by individuals who have no experience in business development.)*

Once you have defined your Dream, Vision, Purpose, and Mission, you will have awakened the entrepreneur within. Now roll up your sleeves and get to work building your business!"

Does this model look vaguely familiar?

I believe for the United States to survive and prosper, we need millions of people to pursue the American Dream through entrepreneurship plus a multiple number of community supporters, mentors, and apprentices. Furthermore, there must be an effective business model through which we can bring this to fruition quickly and incorporate other essential elements that have escaped traditional best practices.

Chapter 17

Rebuild America System™

The PATRIOT MISSION business model actually began to take form when I went *In the Dreaming Room®* as a student in December 2005. I can remember brainstorming with Michael in his office atop the mountains of Petaluma, California as I shared my passion for America and God's blessings in my life. Over the years the prototype took several different forms, but after the countless hours of hard work, trial and error, mentoring, coaching, and field testing, **The PATRIOT MISSION Story** has developed into what I am sharing with you now.

> Our **Dream** is to **LEAD** Americans to Rediscover the "Shining City on a Hill."
>
> Our **Vision** is to **BUILD** a Bold Leadership Team in every County, City, and Parish.
>
> Our **Purpose** is to **GROW** our Capital, Political Influence, and Liberty.
>
> Our **Mission** is to **Rebuild America through the Power of Small Business.**™

Michael has been gracious to serve on our Board of Advisors and continues to offer his candid assessment of the PATRIOT MISSION business model every step of the way. Perhaps you will have the good fortune to hear Michael speak at one of our events or you will get to meet him in one of our Leadership Intensives.

The reason I chose to go into this level of detail is so you understand how PATRIOT MISSION was created. Our model is not based on a theory, but on a cutting edge design that is working for us and countless others.

If you do not have a business, you should be encouraged. You have important skills, talents, ideas, and insights America needs. Regardless of your age, experience, or financial position, there is a way for you to become an entrepreneur if you choose to be. Michael says all you need is a blank piece of paper and a beginner's mind. That does not necessarily mean you have to go out and create an empire, but then again, why not? If you keep an open mind, you will be surprised to discover how valuable your experiences can be to your family, community, marketplace, and nation.

At the same time, while I believe everyone could pursue entrepreneurship, not everyone is called to do so. As we talked about earlier, if we understand and operate in our strengths and talents, we can move mountains together. Regardless of whether you start your own company, entrepreneurial thinking is crucial to mission success. You may be an employee, a stay-at-home mom, a minister, a military member, or a public servant and you are a citizen. America's future will be decided by citizens who support capitalism, become small business apprentices, launch new companies, and mentor entrepreneurs.

Mr. Gerber defines the mission as the task at hand, which in our case is **To Rebuild America through the Power of Small Business**™. To successfully carry out the PATRIOT MISSION, we created the **Rebuild America System**™ to execute three fundamental strategies I call **"the 3 I's."**

Strategy #1—**Inspire** a Nation

Strategy #2—**Implement** Grassroots Chapters

Strategy #3—**Influence** Global Entrepreneurship

By successfully executing each mission strategy, over time we will seamlessly accomplish our Purpose, Vision, and Dream. Each strategy is crafted to support the others and must be technologically connected. Seamless communication from local to national and eventually global levels must be simple and easy for all generations to use. Employing massive, grassroots action in multiple markets as quickly as possible is a key to success.

In subsequent chapters, I will detail how PATRIOT MISSION is executing these three strategies, describe two possible outcomes by 2020, and explain how YOU WIN by helping us. For the moment, let's look at the **3 I's** from a 50,000 foot perch.

Strategy #1—**Inspire** a Nation

To accomplish our massive agenda, people need to be inspired by all that is good in America and motivated to change what is not. The best way to inspire our neighbors in every part of our country is simply to tell America's remarkable story. Depending on a person's generation, hearing these stories of our great country may be like catching up on old times because we have not thought about them in quite some time. However, for many others it will be the first time they have ever heard these powerful anecdotes about our nation and its real history.

As I said in the introduction, this book has been published to inspire you, no matter where you live in America or around the world. Telling **The PATRIOT MISSION Story** is the second step to inspire fellow citizens all over the country because it maps out a pathway to rebuilding our nation.

We must have a healthy respect for our apathetic adversaries and be willing to engage them in order to orchestrate change. We must have powerful reasons to be optimistic about the future and clearly understand the consequences of inaction, which is the reason we continuously ask the question: *"Why Rebuild America?"* In motivational parlance, we are actively pursuing both the pleasure of rebuilding America and avoiding the pain of failing to stop our national demise.

The PATRIOT MISSION Story is a catalyst designed to rekindle optimism which will **LEAD** Americans to Rediscover "The Shining City on a Hill." With over 300 million living Americans and hundreds of millions who have gone before us, there are plenty of stories and reasons we can share with each other. Imagine if only 10% of Americans got inspired!

We often hear the phrase "**We will never forget**" used with respect to 9/11, POWs (prisoners of war), military heroes who made the ultimate sacrifice, and other national tragedies. The problem is, we do forget. We need to be reminded on a regular basis WHY America should be and can be rebuilt. When you merge the **7 Founding LIBERTY Principles** with powerful, personal reasons to save your corner of America, together we can create the highest octane jet fuel necessary to power an entrepreneurial revolution.

Entrepreneurs come from every walk of life and are used to overcoming obstacles. Many have survived tremendous adversity before succeeding. When "survivors" deliver powerful messages that encourage citizens to be proud of America, then we have a fighting chance. This is why the POWER of Your Story is so important. It's one thing to read about historical figures and quite another to hear the powerful testimony of someone who has experienced life in America.

We must overcome politically correct, cultural diversity mantras that seek to marginalize American exceptionalism. As a nation, when we wake up and start to translate our inspiration into action because we remember who we are as a people, then we will have ignited the fuse. Telling these three powerful stories will make that happen:

- America's Story
- **The PATRIOT MISSION Story**
- Your Story

PATRIOT MISSION has organized what we call the **Rebuild America Series**™ to tell these stories in every possible venue, from a personal, 20-minute, one-on-one meeting over coffee, to books, audios, online videos, and live events. Through our PATRIOT MISSION Speakers Bureau, we help facilitate a talented team of passionate professionals who are ready, willing, and able to deliver the message to a nationwide audience.

We have speakers from all industries who are committed to igniting the American entrepreneurial spirit and sharing inspirational messages with a potent call to action. They artfully cross the communication chasm by relating to the Greatest and Silent Generations, Baby Boomers, Gen X, the Millennials and even to our newest Generation Z. Given the scope and pace of our mission, these powerful Speakers Bureau presenters will be busy inspiring and training from sea to shining sea for years to come.

Inspired people within Patriot Community will share our mission, success stories, materials, events, and recognition programs because there will be something in it for them... playing an active role in Rebuilding America! Using advanced technology, we will facilitate and capture national inspiration in many forms and synergistically translate it into hyper-viral growth.

Once you inspire a citizen, you must offer them an action plan that will make a real difference in their everyday life. Otherwise, inspiration without something tangible to do leads to frustration and can quickly become depression. Until now, other than mainly political activities, there has never been a holistic, entrepreneurial system that can make a real difference. We leverage strong, personal inspiration with step-by-step activities that serve the individual and the community; now and for the foreseeable future. This plan's success requires implementing grassroots capitalism.

Strategy #2—<u>Implement</u> Grassroots Chapters

Implementing a PATRIOT MISSION Chapter in each one of 3141 counties, independent cities, and parishes, is how we drive grassroots capitalism deep into the community. Obviously, capitalism and small business have been conducted since the country was founded. Our objective is to use the chapters to capture the growing inspiration from the **Rebuild America Series**™ and use our proprietary systems to create tangible results: **LEAD. BUILD. GROW.**

In its most basic form, the implementation process begins when one person is inspired by the question: *"Why Rebuild America?"* When an entrepreneur, small business owner, supporter of free market capitalism, apprentice, or concerned citizen hears an inspirational message about the "Shining City on a Hill," what happens next? They will share the message with one other person.

When two people share a common passion and have a reason to take action, they tell the story to a third person and invite them to join the effort. Remember the proverb about the cord of three strands which is not easily broken? This is the genesis of how we **BUILD** a Bold Leadership Team in every County, City, and Parish.

The fledgling leadership team metaphorically plants an American flag to mark the local entrepreneurial revolution beachhead. Some leaders may light the fire and tell the story, others will carry the torch into streets and some will be the recruiters; each is crucial in the beginning phase. Grassroots leaders reach out to their networks using every means possible and organize local players to take meaningful action. For you digital natives, a post to your favorite social network will kick-start the local effort. The blueprint implementation is broken down into three short, medium, and long-term programs.

This first implementation program is called **Celebrate Small Business.** It incorporates and adapts the themes of the **Rebuild America Series**™ to the local marketplace. As concerned citizens, entrepreneurs, supporters, job seekers, and the curious begin to plug into the local network, attend events and specialty seminars, they will hear of the inspirational plans to take action in their area. Organizers will invite local pro-small business groups to participate as well.

The community reaches a tipping point when the support, interest, and action meet the necessary benchmarks to launch phase two which is called *The MADE IN THE USA Project*™. This plan actively promotes capitalism and specific small businesses in the local market. The model builds a specific county website promoting local sponsors and encourages the community to shop locally. The project connects with local organizations that support small business in order to unify community-wide efforts. This is important and must be done with care because many groups like Chambers of Commerce can see our project as competition, when in fact just the opposite is true.

The first two implementation phases thank local companies, promote small business, and initiate fledgling entrepreneurial roots in new groups of local citizens. These programs run at least two years. This gives us the time to establish a good working relationship with the local community, which is crucial as we move into the third and long-term phase. The **PATRIOT MISSION Private Business Incubator**™ is a system through which local communities leverage their entrepreneurial experience and active resources to continuously mentor and inspire a new generation of small business professionals.

Different from a traditional bricks and mortar incubator, our focus is connecting all the small business stakeholders in the community with professional resources to help them grow. This includes local colleges and universities who may have physical business incubators as well as entrepreneurship courses. We include angel investors, bankers, and private equity players who are looking for business opportunities.

Implementing thousands of local chapters to develop grassroots capitalism requires a long view of America and a rapid response mentality to drive action now. The common thread to each phase is the **7 Founding LIBERTY Principles**. Opportunists, both individuals and organizations that seek self-enrichment at the expense of others, will not likely be attracted to our programs. When an unprincipled opportunist shows up, they will have the choice to adopt new ways of doing business or to self-deport.

Strategy #3—Influence Global Entrepreneurship

Let me be very clear. America is still the leader of the Free World. We have more freedom to build a business of our own here than anywhere else on the globe. There are tens of millions of global entrepreneurs looking for leadership from America. They are squinting from afar trying to see the flickering light atop the hill, although the dark clouds make it hard to discern a once great city.

We influence global small businesses when we set a good example, both personally and technologically. By growing our capital, political influence, and liberty at home, we inspire others to pursue freedom in their lands. Strong foreign policy encourages people from the four corners of the Earth to become more productive and stretch for our markets. Some may choose to apply to emigrate and legally live here where they can see the "Shining City on a Hill" much more closely.

Global commerce is interconnected in many ways. We can conduct business via the Internet with anyone around the world that is holding a smart phone. We can create new markets for our products and services as well as learn from international partners who have a lot to offer. As entrepreneurs, we can joint venture with service providers, manufacturers, and technology specialists on countless platforms in record time to upgrade our products and services. We need to leverage global opportunities when it makes sense.

Our continued influence in the world depends on how well we, as individual Americans, take responsibility for our current state of affairs. I believe if we passionately inspire a national entrepreneurial revolution and quickly execute at the grassroots level, we can have a major impact at home and abroad. We will inspire the world by reaffirming America's founding principles and cranking up the fracking derived, natural-gas-powered streetlamps to light up our hilltop city.

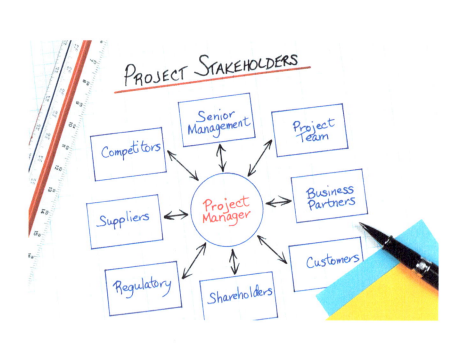

Chapter 18

Stakeholders and Execution Plan

PATRIOT MISSION Stakeholders

We need inspired Americans representing broad demographic groups in every community to step up, band together and go to work to execute these three strategies. In the balance of this chapter, I will broadly define who these stakeholders are, their motivations, and the key roles they play in our functional plan. In the remaining chapters I'll explain how national inspiration sparks practical implementation at the grassroots level and eventually influences global entrepreneurship.

> DEFINITION: **Stakeholder**—*noun*—a person or group that has an investment, share, or interest in something, as a business or industry.[16]

The popular definition refers to an interest in "something." Some of us are stakeholders in a business we founded and others have a stake where they are employed. As an employee, you might not have an equity interest, but you certainly have a personal interest in helping the company succeed. The same is true of government at multiple levels. As citizens or legal residents, we are stakeholders in our local town, county, state, and nation. The taxes we pay on income, property, intangibles, capital gains, businesses. and our death, prove it.

We define PATRIOT MISSION stakeholders in order to effectively serve each demographic with programs, services, products, and referrals to partner organizations. As you read through the four broadly defined roles, you may identify with a primary and secondary role. Your role changes over time depending on where you are in life's journey.

The stakeholders are listed in order of the size of the group in an average county, city, or parish. For example, there are more **Supporters** than **Founders** and more **Founders** than **Mentors** in a community. To keep the descriptions simple, I've painted each using a picture of the stakeholder's primary motivations.

Supporter—You love our country and want to help preserve our liberty and freedom. You are frustrated by many issues and are looking for practical ways to make a difference. You are connected to a fair number of people and are likely to be politically active. You are not looking for a new business venture but you do support capitalism in your area, state-wide and nationally.

Founder—You lead a small business venture. It's likely you were the original owner or you may have bought the business to grow and expand. Your time and resources are limited. You want to find creative ways to help the country while promoting your business to a local, regional, and perhaps national audience. Increasing company income, profit, and equity are primary motivators.

Mentor—You have talents, skills, and experience you would like to invest in others. You may be a Founder moving toward succession planning; perhaps you are retired or are an active employee. Your heart is to serve others. Time is precious. You want to make a difference and see the impact on others. You may be an angel investor and open to entertain synergistic business opportunities.

Apprentice—You may be a recent college or high school graduate looking for a job. You may be a more senior worker who has been downsized, underutilized, or are concerned about what's coming over the horizon. You may be coming back to the workforce or seeking more household income.

This following stakeholder is different from the other four. The partner position is central to the **PATRIOT MISSION** business model and may be filled by any of the other stakeholders, depending on their qualifications, interest, experience, time availability, resources, and personal motivations.

Partner—The PATRIOT MISSION Story resonates and you want to be part of inspiring a nation and implementing grassroots capitalism. Your skill sets will vary depending on your experience. You may have executive, marketing, sales, training, social media, management, writing and/or speaking skills. You are open to leadership or business development opportunities.

You want to have a direct relationship with **PATRIOT MISSION** and use your talents, skills, and gifts productively within the local, state, regional, or national business model. You may wish to add new revenue streams to your company or make a career transition with a substantial income upgrade. You may be early in your career and have an unbridled enthusiasm to help promote this message. You may wish to donate potential earnings to the PATRIOT Grant Program or a third party charity of your choice.

These broad stakeholder roles help orient and move us in a direction that makes the best use of your time and keeps the organization mission focused. Although we are discussing each of these stakeholders as individuals, they also represent organizations whose purposes are analogous to an individual's motivations. As you will see in *The **MADE IN THE USA Project***™, we invite both individuals and organizations to participate so we create maximum impact in a community. We expect to have many synergist relationships with Partner companies.

PATRIOT MISSION National Leadership Team

Effective leadership at local, regional, and national levels of the organization is the key to our success. By building a strong core leadership team comprised of partners with diverse expertise, we can quickly accomplish our goals. We will invite qualified candidates to join our national leadership team based on their passion for our mission, participation in our strategic programs, personal goals and experience.

Members of the National Leadership Team will represent all the stakeholder roles and include those who are active in a local chapter. Most members will also be partners in one of many different specialties. There will be merit based incentives for the National Leadership Team based on how members impact the organization at large.

PATRIOT MISSION National Speakers Bureau

While many people rank public speaking among their biggest fears, there are those who embrace the challenge of communicating from the stage, whether at a public event, webinar, radio show, or on television. Our speaking team will represent all five stakeholder profiles. This will include the professionally trained and certified speakers and a second group of approved presenters who will share topical, educational, and expert messages based on their personal knowledge and experience.

PATRIOT MISSION certified speakers are partners who have been trained to professionally deliver programs which are part of our **Rebuild America Series**™. They weave in their personal experiences to present a compelling, motivating, and action oriented message. This is a strong, diverse team of presenters who ignite the entrepreneurial spirit and inspire local, regional, and national audiences. As a speaking team, they are skilled at edifying others and connecting with multiple market segments.

Supporters, Founders, Mentors, and Apprentices comprise the second group because each of these stakeholders can effectively communicate unique experiences to those of similar profiles. These may be credentialed experts in any number of fields including business, finance, faith, history, military leadership, education, small business, political science, and other topics. In other cases, our members may have a unique and valuable perspective on an issue to share with the audience.

Combining certified speakers who are trained to facilitate audience interaction with passionate team members delivering real stories and topical insights is powerful. This strategy paves the way for a constant flow of new speakers who learn how to tell their stories and get experience in front of audiences to build enough confidence to go through certification training. Over the coming years, our professional speakers will be featured in every imaginable venue.

As you'll see, much of the grassroots training will start in small groups learning to tell stories, beginning with the story you know best... yours.

5 <u>MILES</u> to Rebuild America System™ Implementation

In coordination with the national leadership team and its Partners, PATRIOT MISSION uses a five-step pattern to implement each business development strategy. We've listed the five sequential pattern steps below to give you a very brief idea how the system works as we grow nationally, regionally, and locally. We use the acronym **MILES** to keep it simple.

1. **MAP**—Map the tactical action plan for the next program. Use the operating templates to customize the steps based on the resources, economic status, etc., of national, regional, or local marketplace. Determine the size of the leadership team necessary to support this implementation phase to promote capitalism and support small businesses.

2. **IGNITE**—Ignite inspiration and build pre-launch momentum for this phase by sharing stories of small business members and key leaders. Connect with each stakeholder group and educate them using the program materials which are relevant to them. Ask questions and listen. Spark "brushfires" so people in the local marketplace will come from miles around to watch you burn.

3. **LAUNCH**—Launch the next programmed phase of the **Rebuild America System**™ when kickoff criteria are met. Prepare your partner team to professionally serve local, regional, and national members and gather feedback using system tools during the entire launch sequence.

4. **ENGAGE**—Engage with stakeholders to determine how well the program phase is meeting the goals and

objectives for each group. Immerse as effectively as possible to get real time feedback and submit observations, suggestions, and ideas for continuous improvement to national leadership and PATRIOT MISSION team.

5. **SUSTAIN**—Sustain operational excellence during each program plan deliverable. As each phase matures, keep a close watch for complacency and mediocrity. Maintain aggressive attention to detail as you work with your team to MAP the next program phase.

MISSION ACCOMPLISHED?

How long will David need to take out Goliath?
I contend the timeline will largely depend on how efficiently, effectively, and rapidly the National Leadership Team executes our American Entrepreneurial Revolution. If we hustle and work hard, in a few short years we can make significant progress on our privately funded "Shining City on a Hill" rehab project.

Measuring direct results in terms of participants, county expansion, and reported business growth are important to benchmark progress toward mission accomplishment. Although the metrics are more subjective, we will also track the growth of our capital, political influence, and liberty.

Now that you know what the three mission critical strategies are, I will detail how they function and who does the work. Then I'll offer two **2020 Storyline** options and you can decide what part of the blueprint you want to focus on.

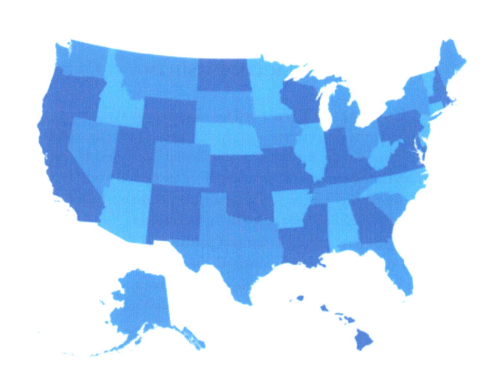

Chapter 19

Strategy #1—Inspire a Nation

Throughout history, nations have been inspired by stories passed down through the generations. America's history is a powerful motivator for me. Before we get too deep in this chapter, I want to put something on the table that may be nagging at you. I want to state for the record, I understand how audacious and perhaps arrogant it may sound for me to suggest **The PATRIOT MISSION Story** can inspire a nation. When we look back at the great societal movements, I can understand why some may believe this idea is way over the top. I would like to refer you back to the birth of **The PATRIOT MISSION Story** on January 16, 2011. Remember the vision I shared with you?

I am very clear there is no way in my human flesh I could lead this effort. While I have had my successes, I could write an entire series of books on my mistakes. My job is to be obedient and listen to the still small voice inside me. Philippians 4:13 tells me I can do all things through Christ who gives me strength. I will apply everything I have learned to build a great team and carry out the vision.

Whether you agree with my personal spiritual perspective isn't the issue. Here's where I hope we can agree. It will take an act of God and His favor on our team to **Inspire a Nation** and expeditiously Rebuild America for this and future generations. When we get to the end of this story, you can decide if you are called to join me and play a role, or not.

How will the Rebuild America System™ Inspire an entire nation?

For starters, we don't think about inspiring a country. We start by inspiring one person. Inspiration is an emotion that is felt in one beating heart. That's where we begin. How do we touch one of our fellow citizens in such a way that he would be moved to listen to more stories? Once she gets enthused about what she's heard, how do we help her stay engaged? Those are the questions.

Let's take a brief look at the math. In America today, there are over 300 million citizens. How many people do we need to inspire and engage in order to make a difference? Our goal is 10% of the population (including kids) in the next seven years, which equates to 30 million people; one out of every ten citizens in America. I know... you can stop laughing. Again, we don't start by trying to recruit 30 million people to become inspired entrepreneurial revolutionaries or supportive capitalists; we start with a few patriots in each county.

In an average county of 100,000 people, what if we could inspire one out of a hundred? That's only 1% or in this example, 1000 folks. Now that's not beyond comprehension over the course of a year or two, is it? I don't think so. What happens over the course of a few years, when we encourage an average of 1000 people in 3141 counties? That's over three million people or 10% of our goal. See, not that difficult, is it? Give it a few more years and we meet our goal. No sweat.

I know; the math always works. My point is with a goal, good strategy, a strong team, and Divine Providence, we can get the job done. It is harder to grow from 100 to 10,000 than it will be to go from 3 to 30 million. As stories grow rapidly in many areas, momentum will grow exponentially.

Strategy #1—<u>Inspire</u> a Nation — 165

Who can be inspired?

People who are looking for a way to be successful are typically open to inspiration. As a matter of fact, they are looking for it. What many folks really want is just a way to make money and provide for their families. At the core of their being, whether they realize it or not, people want to know there is a real opportunity for them to live a productive life. We are sharing a grassroots message of real hope wrapped up in an invitation to learn, grow, and work. It's been said opportunity is often dressed in small business work clothes.

The people who have already made up their minds they want to be wards of the state and live off free government benefits are not our primary target in the early stages. If those guys are ever to be inspired, they will only make a move if their benefits disappear or if someone they respect challenges them. I've read studies about the huge percentage of people who never read a book after high school. It is likely the only way they will ever be inspired to learn is to see or hear a story about someone like them who got fired up and changed their life for the better. Even then it's 50/50; remember the bushel of crabs.

Getting folks revved up based on false hope is cruel. Unfortunately, it happens all too frequently. Look at the lottery. It doesn't take much to get people fantasizing about how they would spend their newfound wealth. It's certainly easy to pick your lucky numbers, gamble a few bucks, and hope for a miracle. It's harder to save those hard-earned dollars and invest your capital in a plan for the future built around your strengths. It can be even harder to stare down peer pressure.

Another major hurdle we must overcome is effectively delivering inspiration over the noise of everyday life. What does that mean? Think about how much true quiet time there is in a day; time without any background noise or media distraction. When you turn on television, radio, social media, YouTube, or anything else on the Internet, you are bombarded with marketing messages. This creates mental saturation and limits the brain's processing power. Most people have a tough time being inspired about anything when they are completely maxed out mentally.

Think about your computer hard drive. How well does it operate when it is above 95% full? It doesn't work well at all. Memory starts to shut down, programs stop working and the computer begins to run only essential functions. That's exactly what happens to us if we do not leave time in our day or room in our brain to take in new ideas. This is the starting point of our inspirational journey across America. There are two broad divisions in the marketplace of ideas; those who do not immediately value our message and others who start jumping up and down when they hear it.

Infusing our message into people who don't recognize its value initially requires multiple delivery methods, diverse stories, and patience. Unless we share something they want and are motivated to consume, the message gets deleted. They need to receive real, inspirational stories from people they know, trust, and like. They know in their gut America is in a bind, but have no idea what to do. Over time, our message will sink in and gain priority in their lives because they are burned out. They want to hear more stories and learn how this optimism can lead to a better life for them.

Fortunately, there is also a large subset of the American marketplace that is actively looking for **The PATRIOT MISSION Story**. Of course, they do not know it by name but they are searching for a solution. How do I know this to be true? As I have traveled around the country since 2011 sharing this idea, these people immediately smile and ask me how they can help. I can't tell you how many times I have heard people tell me things like: *"This is awesome, I was hoping someone would do something like this! How can I get involved?"*

Look at some of the most popular, prime-time television shows that promote entrepreneurship or DIY (do it yourself) programs about everything from flipping real estate to making cupcakes. There are shows about bosses who have a heart to serve their customers and employees while making a nice profit. If the audience did not want to see these shows, they would be off the air because advertisers would drop like flies.

What about talk radio listeners? How many of the top, long running programs have messages that are congruent with **The PATRIOT MISSION Story**? A lot. Some of these shows have TENS OF MILLIONS of listeners, many of whom are frustrated. After the information is delivered to their brain, they rarely get specific, step-by-step guidance on how to change the situation. Typically the shows' purposes are entertainment and education. The frustration is compounded by the fact a majority of program content relates to high level political, economic, or legal issues, which most people don't believe they can impact directly.

Then of course you have tens of millions of people at any given second engaging in social media, blogs, news aggregators, flash reporting, and online television. In this medium, people can engage because they can share their comments and perspectives. People feel emboldened here to reveal their true feelings because they can pick an anonymous avatar and tell the world what they really think. This can be a real eye-opener.

This is why I know there are at least 30 million to 50 million people who, over time, will hear about **The PATRIOT MISSION Story**. They are looking for inspiration with a game plan attached to it. You can read their calls for help in their online comments and in the questions they ask radio show hosts. Certainly there are a healthy percentage of online lurkers ranting in the shadows who will never lift a finger to solve the problem. That's fine, they can entertain themselves. In the meantime, for those who want to help and WIN in the process, we will focus our attention on helping translate their frustration into inspiration and ultimately into grassroots capitalism; county-by-county.

If you are personally inspired by the ideas in this book, then we have accomplished the first step. Once an inspirational seed is planted, it must be watered and nurtured to grow and multiply. Inspiration is infectious and can grow virally. You might start by simply sharing this book with one other person in your home, town, state, or perhaps across the country. You may or may not be in a position to do more than that, but it is important for you to know there is always a place to turn. You are part of the solution and can plug in anytime to help us continue the mission. As we walk through the balance of the book, you'll discover how you can translate your inspiration into effective action.

What type of inspiration is productive?

Rarely does inspiration occur through a cerebral lecture or an educational program. Lasting inspiration typically happens when someone experiences a personal epiphany. It can happen in an instant. Stories are often be the catalyst to inspire people at a deep, emotional level. Inspiration can become the motivation for a person to take action and change their life. It is all about them. The inspiration we share must serve each person, individually.

Frequently, we do not know when we have inspired someone because they go through a step-by-step metamorphosis themselves. They start to feel and see things from a new point of view. They take the first steps to chart a new course for their future and begin to make personal changes. There must be a continual flow of stories, events, and support for newly inspired people to remain on track.

Inspiring stories are easy to remember and pass on to others. Most people can recall the story of David and Goliath, even if they learned it in Sunday school as a kid. Stories of people who are winning in life are fun to tell, especially when we can see ourselves in the story. People believe stories they hear from others who are most like them. This is one of the reasons eventually we will offer stories from every generation, from the most senior to the youngest and everything in between. Our stories will celebrate true American heritage.

We will recognize small business success and prove rags to riches experiences are still possible, despite the bureaucratic nightmare we face. We need stories to validate hard work and creativity. Real stories illuminate American Exceptionalism and destroy the myths of socialism. These true powerhouse experiences can inspire trapped Americans to break the dependency cycle and step into grassroots capitalism. When people get inspired and take a single positive step to improve their life, it builds the confidence to take another step. Walking this lifelong journey toward success is not just for people who have lived in poverty or faced tough times.

You and I both need inspiration. We need to know what we do matters. We need to be motivated to get out of bed in the morning and be productive citizens. Our families need to believe in us and what we are contributing to society. Millions of people still want to believe in America, but are losing hope. Inspiration is the encouragement we need to LEAD ourselves as well as others to rediscover the "Shining City on a Hill." We encourage you to focus on what you do best because YOU WIN by pursuing your strengths, talents, and passions. America wins when YOU WIN.

Do you get inspired when you see the U.S. flag waving in the breeze? Do you get goose bumps when you hear the Star Spangled Banner? I still do. I think it's safe to say, most Americans over the age of 10 probably know the first stanza of our national anthem. Here's something you may not know. In last line of the first stanza, Francis Scott Key actually asks a question;

> *"Oh, say does that star-spangled banner yet wave*
> *O'er the land of the free and the home of the brave?"*

As a prisoner, he peers through the small opening overlooking the Chesapeake Bay and finds the large flag still flying over Fort McHenry. At first Key is inspired by what he thinks he sees. He is hopeful his eyes are not playing tricks on him... is that enormous flag still flying?

In the remaining three verses, the question transitions to a bold, confident statement because he knows the Americans repelled the British attack. This is precisely what happens to us when inspiration is followed by a story we can confirm is true. We become confident and BOLD.

If you are like me, it may have been a decade or two since you reflected on the depth and meaning of all the words in this iconic song. For a minute, imagine you are sitting next to Francis Scott Key watching the bombardment of Fort McHenry during that long night in the War of 1812. Feel the emotions in his words:

> Oh, say can you see by the dawn's early light
> What so proudly we hailed at the twilight's last gleaming?
> Whose broad stripes and bright stars through the perilous fight,
> O'er the ramparts we watched were so gallantly streaming?
> And the rockets' red glare, the bombs bursting in air,
> Gave proof through the night that our flag was still there.
> <u>Oh, say does that star-spangled banner yet wave</u>
> <u>O'er the land of the free and the home of the brave?</u>
>
> On the shore, dimly seen through the mists of the deep,
> Where the foe's haughty host in dread silence reposes,
> What is that which the breeze, o'er the towering steep,
> As it fitfully blows, half conceals, half discloses?

Now it catches the gleam of the morning's first beam,
In full glory reflected now shines in the stream:
<u>'Tis the star-spangled banner! Oh long may it wave</u>
<u>O'er the land of the free and the home of the brave!</u>

And where is that band who so vauntingly swore
That the havoc of war and the battle's confusion,
A home and a country should leave us no more!
Their blood has washed out their foul footsteps' pollution.
No refuge could save the hireling and slave
From the terror of flight, or the gloom of the grave:
<u>And the star-spangled banner in triumph doth wave</u>
<u>O'er the land of the free and the home of the brave!</u>

Oh! thus be it ever, when freemen shall stand
Between their loved home and the war's desolation!
Blest with victory and peace, may the heav'n rescued land
Praise the Power that hath made and preserved us a nation.
Then conquer we must, when our cause it is just,
And this be our motto: **"In God is our trust."**
<u>And the star-spangled banner in triumph shall wave</u>
<u>O'er the land of the free and the home of the brave!</u>

This became our national anthem by congressional decree on March 3, 1931. I wonder if it had to be voted on today, whether it would get beyond the political correctness crowd since the second to last sentence emphatically states our country's motto: "In God is our trust." We'll save that discussion for another time.

Oftentimes, the military and first responders are referred to in this verse, which is certainly fitting. But the fact of the matter is that each citizen has a responsibility to be one of the brave if they expect to have a homeland that is free.

Here's my question.

How many citizens do you think believe if we are to remain a free country, they will have to become one of the brave people to whom Francis Scott Key is referring?

I dare say, if you hired a polling firm to survey the number of people willing to publicly declare themselves one of *"the brave,"* the numbers would be painfully low. Even if the definition of brave did not require going to war, becoming a cop or fighting fires, how many Americans will fight for our national freedom in the trenches of the marketplace?

Many would respond: *"That's not my job; the military and first responders handle bravery issues and politicians deal with economic issues."* There's the problem. My fellow Americans, we are the first responders to protect our families, homes, businesses, and liberty. There are over 300 million of us and we must be responsible to value and protect our freedom. If we don't, who will?

We cannot delegate bravery. A discouraged, beaten-down populous will not stand up and fight for our freedom or liberty. America needs those who can look upon Lady Liberty in New York Harbor and get inspired. She needs citizens who hear the sound of freedom when a four ship of fighter jets roar overhead in full afterburner. Who will stand with us?

Only the brave who understand what it means to live in a free land will stand with us. We must increase our numbers and do it quickly or tyranny will continue to expand and we will lose what's left of our freedom. Fortunately, we do not need an armed insurrection to win this battle in the marketplace of ideas and commerce. That's how they do it in banana republics.

Chapter 20

The Impact of America's New Founders

The New Founders and their Teammates

Our nation's founders made decisions that changed world history. At this moment in time, those of us who have or will **FOUND** a small business are making a potentially momentous decision. While we may not be starting a new nation, a founder's decision at this moment in history comes with major consequences. While we may not be staring down the barrel of a musket or standing on the edge of the gallows, I believe the future of our constitutional republic will be determined by those of us who understand the real stakes and stand in the gap.

When you found an entrepreneurial venture, whether you realize it or not, you are volunteering to Rebuild America. At first, you may only see it as a financial decision to make a few extra bucks. However, when you grasp the potential impact on your family, employees, contractors, vendors, clients, community, state, country, and perhaps the world, the decision becomes much bigger.

It's easy to say, *"I'm one of the 22 million sole proprietors and my business isn't going to change the country."* That is a matter of opinion. In the old paradigm, it is likely you could operate your business as a disconnected entity that lived or died without anyone noticing. In our updated view, your business gets plugged into a support system that wants you to succeed and energizes you with ideas, connections, and resources to help you thrive, even in the face of challenges.

Our military, law enforcement, and emergency personnel volunteer to go into harm's way every day and we applaud their service. They too have volunteered to follow their passion and a calling to serve. As Small Business FOUNDERS, we must decide to be the brave marketplace leaders our country must have if we are to Rebuild America. As entrepreneurs, we can touch the lives of so many people and by simply understanding and embracing the impact of our decision to FOUND a company, we take the critical first steps.

They are the nearly 30 million entrepreneurs and small business owners across America.

That's an average of about 9500 per county. What do you think will happen when 100 or 1000 of those 9500 in each county, independent city, and parish begin to claim their position as FOUNDERS, not simply as little small business guys trying to get down the road and survive? There is power in the decisions we make and in the people with whom we choose to associate.

While Founders play a leading role in the local marketplace, it is also important to understand how important the other three primary stakeholders are to the Founders and the economy. It may seem obvious the Supporters are important because they represent the largest group of retail consumers. They also play a key role in citizen support for free-enterprise-friendly legislation which makes the Founders' businesses viable.

A majority of mentors have small business experience as Founders themselves or have medium to large corporate experience. They have specialized skill sets which can tremendously accelerate Founders' innovation. Imagine being an apprentice in position to observe, learn, and participate as these three groups interfaced. Then when the apprentice thinks he is ready to explore the wisdom of launching a new idea into the marketplace, he delivers his pitch in front of a ready panel of potential customers, business associates, and angel investors. That's why we call it a team.

It is hard to underestimate the challenges we face in America today.

As leaders, when we get inspired, we can **Inspire a Nation**. Small Business Founders are the dependable soul of the community. In many ways we too serve as first responders. We generate the money to pay the military, police, fire rescue, and emergency teams. If it weren't for The New Founders, we would just have tribes and gangs wandering the streets like one-third of the rest of the world.

If we need any extra inspiration, all we have to do is read history. Fortunately, we have a long list of brave Founders and leaders who have gone before us. Their stories of bravery and commitment are immense. Patrick Henry expressed their sentiment well: "***Give me Liberty or Death.***" Our country's founders knew exactly what was on the line when they penned their names on the Declaration of Independence... and interestingly, many of the 56 signers were businessmen.

> *"Where there is no vision, the people perish."*
> —Proverbs **29.18**

Unless we ignite inspiration in America quickly, people will rapidly lose any hope in the future. If Americans have no vision of a good life or at least a better life for their kids and grandkids, then what is the point? Are we just here to exist until we return to dust? No.

Leaders take Inspiration to the streets of America.
It will take people from all walks of life, in every part of America to inspire our fellow citizens. In the early stages, it will take pioneers from each stakeholder profile that hear **The PATRIOT MISSION Story** and share our **7 Founding LIBERTY Principles** to step up and take the lead. These leaders will champion the message and cast an inspirational vision within their circles of influence.

Ultimately, it will take an organized, professional team of dedicated people who will balance their appropriate self-interest with the critical mission at hand. Across our great land, we are building a talent pool of gifted communicators to deliver inspirational messages intertwined with a strong call to action to audiences large and small.

Igniting Inspiration at Events

During our discussion on growing personal capital, I talked about experiential education and its impact on our lives. PATRIOT MISSION will sponsor ongoing events in many different formats. These inspirational programs will have several common elements including fun, networking, travel, and time to relax. Traveling to attend a boring conference is a drag. Who wants to get on a plane, sit in a meeting room, eat hotel food, listen to lectures for days on end and fly home?

> *"If you light yourself on fire, people will come from miles around to watch you burn."*

This is a lesson I learned in one my first sales trainings while I was transitioning from the Air Force into the world of entrepreneurship. An experienced motivational speaker taught me if you are going to sell an idea, especially a new concept, you have to be willing to put yourself out in the city square and share your message with passion. Successful events evoke heartfelt inspiration, a strong message, and a powerful delivery.

Our events will combine learning with adventure and time to hear your fellow patriots' stories. Developing new relationships while sharing common experiences can be a powerful way to create new stories that are great to share, especially when people are from difference places across the country and are cross-generational. Creating new legends is fun and unique.

It's safe to say, our plans include events in international waters on dedicated PATRIOT MISSION cruise ships as well as special trips around the world to key historical locations.

Inspiration Impact

Have you ever been in a very challenging situation that seemed hopeless? I've been there, you probably have as well. Unless you are under five years old, we've all faced times that are bruisers. You had to deal with what appeared to be an insurmountable obstacle.

Perhaps you exhausted every resource you could think of to solve the problem. You were at the end of your rope and didn't know what to do next. Maybe you cried out to God for a miracle or simply stared off into the emptiness of space wondering what would come of the situation.

Then something happened... a person, an idea, a voice, or maybe a full-blown miracle. That something was an inspiration at a time when you needed it most. America needs inspiration right now and it won't come from outside, it must come from within.

For those of us who agree with the Founder's perspective on Divine Providence, we know we must humble ourselves before God and ask for his inspiration. When we do, I believe he will heal our land. One thing is certain. When we are inspired and share true, heartfelt belief with another person, our collective faith can move mountains.

Our conviction to **Rebuild America through the Power of Small Business**™ is contagious.

Rebuild America System™ Infrastructure
(No government stimulus cash required)

Implementing grassroots capitalism in 3141 counties, independent cities, and parishes in less than seven years requires organization, a well designed game plan, and substantial infrastructure. Technology gives us the ability to quickly share with others' smart phones, computers, and televisions. We will use existing platforms and emerging technologies to share our point of view directly with audiences of every generation and geography.

This support structure is crucial so people can stay plugged in and connected to everything that is happening in real time.

There are many online systems that can capture and rapidly share inspirational moments, too. Think about the immediate impact of sharing stories. Many times, inspiration can come in the simplest form. A colleague's victory or a heart wrenching plea for help can ignite a fire. It may be through a picture, quote, short story, or a video. We will compile stories in easy-to-digest formats to infuse inspiration directly into the grassroots.

The intellectual firepower of generational experience multiplied by the technological horsepower of younger citizens creates great opportunity. To engage stakeholders at every level, we combine social media applications with "old school" technology, like books and face-to-face events.

Humans still have a need to see each other and interact. Our format bolsters effective personal communication, which is becoming a lost art that needs to be salvaged. Implementing a cross-generational, multi-media communication platform is crucial because we need to reach the four corners of every local marketplace.

Rebuild America Series™

Our signature subscription series of ongoing educational information and orientation presentations designed to inspire people with America's Story, **The PATRIOT MISSION Story**, and your story. The introductory programs and stories in the series are usually the initial seeds that begin to take root in a person's mind and spirit. The subscriber's primary benefit is inspiration, access to PATRIOT MISSION resources, and the opportunity to plug into our team events and meet others.

Series presentations are delivered in multiple formats including webcast, teleconference, and live events. Programs are normally delivered by certified PATRIOT MISSION Speakers Bureau professionals in multiple channels to plant grassroots seeds in each stakeholder demographic. We continuously add to our library of presentation materials for delivery to growing and diverse audiences. The series will also include interactive specialty sessions with attendees to engage the audience on relevant topics that matter to them.

Each program will include an invitation to join or to start a local group which could become a PATRIOT MISSION chapter. Participants are also invited to bring resources to the table to educate our membership about products, services, or a point of view that will serve the organization at large.

Much of the information and the stories in the **Rebuild America Series**™ will come from the "new founders." This group's passions, decisions, commitments, and risk are the bold, driving force behind our capability to inspire the nation and implement grassroots capitalism chapters.

The POWER of Small Business™

The POWER of Small Business™ is an ever-expanding collection of inspirational stories told from the first person perspective. These are your stories of trial and triumph. Our fellow Americans are looking for leadership and encouragement. They want to get to know people who have experienced a "real" entrepreneurial life, which many people relate to the American Dream. The key to inspiring a nation in record time is to connect with individual people at a heart level. It will be your stories that spark the connection.

When you are willing to share a part of your life story describing a painful, hopeful, triumphant, or expectant experience, you can have a huge impact on someone. Think about the stories you have heard over your lifetime that have inspired you. Many times, it's not the famous stories that everyone has heard from media, platform stages, or the movies.

Our stories of persistence, drive, focus, recovery, stress, excitement, success, and struggle will paint an inspirational picture in the mind's eye of each and every person who hears our stories. When our stories are delivered in an organized format with the tangible action steps we map out in **The PATRIOT MISSION Story**, we can rapidly build positive momentum across the country.

Inspiring a nation is a worthy strategy provided there is a direct connection to action. Now, let's talk about how we bring this inspiration to life through the second mission critical strategy in the **Rebuild America System™**, which is to **<u>Implement</u> Grassroots Chapters**.

Chapter 21

Stragegy #2—Implement Grassroots Chapters

As I travel across America, people often ask me exactly what we do at PATRIOT MISSION. In the simplest terms, we promote capitalism and support local small businesses. We are also professional storytellers who aim to invigorate supporters, recharge founders, encourage mentors, and inspire a new generation of entrepreneurs to get in the game. We endorse working together to save America from a destiny of laziness, apathy, corruption, excess government, and bankruptcy.

In the previous chapter, I outlined why we must light the fire of inspiration in the hearts of men and women across the USA. We discussed how we promote entrepreneurship and small business through our national **Rebuild America Series**™ using various event and media channels. Finally, we touched on the need to make best use of technology and support systems to make this happen on a fast moving, local, regional, and national scale. We now turn our attention to the point where the proverbial rubber hits the road.

Translating Inspiration into Productive Action

We've all had mountaintop experiences that stoke our fires with a powerful message; however, when inspiration is not immediately connected with meaningful action, the impact is usually short-lived. This means national inspiration must seep into the fabric of our daily lives and take root in every county, city, and parish. The inspiration fueled road trip we are on to save America must translate into ongoing activities that produce supportive communities, innovative small businesses, coached upstarts, new jobs, and strong financials.

Furthermore, our unique grassroots strategy must go to work in the face of stiff marketplace and bureaucratic headwinds. The upside is evident when our fellow citizens grow their personal and professional capital. They get stronger and bolder. Their influence on local, regional, and national ballot box races becomes clearer and more pronounced when public servants are hired. Real GDP grows and national debt drops if public servants embrace our **7 Founding LIBERTY Principles.**

Our system incorporates the universal theme of Rebuilding America, which expands and matures over years. For participants, it will become deeply personal and will impact their family for generations to come.

The resultant impact on the local community over time is a broad return to our founder's vision for the USA. When we leverage our work with synergistic efforts by fellow Patriots who share our passion for America, we can rehabilitate the "Shining City on a Hill" one citizen, one county, one city, and one parish at a time.

The system must profitably serve an ever-changing group of people who pursue their goals and move in and out of the area. For long-term participants, the system must deliver a perpetually meaningful experience with enough flexibility to adapt to local interests and heritage.

Without these systemic characteristics, all we could do is inspire people and hope they figure out what to do with their newfound motivation. This would just create another flash in the pan, feel-good message that fades away with little or no results. Unless we capture and hold people's attention, they will run after the next shiny object in two seconds flat, which would be a colossal waste of time and resources. The stakes are too high to miss our target.

We must produce an attractive storyline to rekindle the hearts and minds of the American people to re-embrace liberty and freedom before 2020. This storyline must become tangible in the community and in the hearts and minds of local citizens. Only when words are applied in meaningful action will an ever growing, cynical population believe there is truth in our message. The good news is we don't have to make up a new story. We are inviting millions of our fellow citizens to experience America's story through the eyes of patriotic entrepreneurs and supporters.

Implementing Grassroots Capitalism: County-by-County

Each of the 3141 counties, independent cities, and parishes will be represented by at least one PATRIOT MISSION Chapter. Think of your local chapter as a giant puzzle. These separate, disjointed pieces are yearning for connection. Each puzzle piece and the silver shadow below represent individual and organizational stakeholders' perspectives.

In most counties, there are substantial resources many people do not know exist and often go unused. Typically, if each organization's resources were coordinated synergistically with the others, their combined overall value would far surpass their individual impact. As you'll see, our model is designed to pull these people and groups together to promote their individual value and strengthen the community impact.

Implementing this franchise-like chapter model leverages technology and support requirements to keep operating costs low while increasing member access to national resources outside of the local area. Operational standardization is critical because it means local chapter members can focus on what is most important to them, not managing support infrastructure.

With every new county chapter that comes on line, we learn a host of lessons which are woven into the continuously improving operating systems. As best practices emerge and key metrics are refined, the **Rebuild America System**™ is updated to reflect new standards. These improvements are then seamlessly incorporated in each independent, licensed chapter.

Local chapters are launched when grassroots interests meet specific criteria based on the county demographics and economy. We have designed three sequential programs that educate, engage, and support the community. My intention now is to help you understand the big picture for each program and show you how they cascade into their successor over time. You can consult our resource materials for the most current program updates and chapter locations.

Developing the Patriot Community on a Solid Foundation

PATRIOT MISSION designed three implementation modules to broadly, effectively, and profitably drive grassroots capitalism deep into the fabric of communities nationwide. Each of these cascading programs has a turnkey execution plan with benchmarks and timelines for each chapter:

1. **Celebrate Small Business**™
2. *The MADE IN THE USA Project*™
3. **Private Business Incubator**™

Each program builds a solid foundation to support the next and balances stakeholder interests with a sound financial model to ensure long-term marketplace viability. We use the term cascading because each successive program plants seeds that grow in the next phase. For example, as we **Celebrate Small Business**™, we prepare the local area for *The MADE IN THE USA Project*™, which builds support for the **Private Business Incubator**™.

To be a successful grassroots model, each local stakeholder must have the opportunity to take ownership of the process without being overwhelmed. Since time is our most precious commodity, we must value each person's time and ensure each offer serves their best interests. We encourage all stakeholders to contribute ideas, insights, and suggestions along the way.

As the inspired Patriot Community grows in the USA, our support system metrics will help us determine which county chapters to open up next. This makes the best use of resources and leverages inspiration to **Celebrate Small Business**™, where it is most likely to spark a new citywide grassfire.

We also believe it is crucial for local leaders who are championing the implementation to participate in the decision-making process for each phase. As local leaders work with partners to open a new chapter, every step of the first program is coordinated with our support team as it comes on line. This ensures strong mission continuity during the transition from virtual to local.

Capital Growth Cycle

You will recall the PATRIOT MISSION Purpose is to **GROW** our Capital, Political Influence, and Liberty. Earlier I described in detail the macro elements of personal and professional capital (see chart above) and the general strategies we employ to develop them.

The Capital Growth Cycle is the operating model that combines stakeholders' personal and professional capital goals with three action-based programs to produce results. From an operational viewpoint, this cycle is like an electromagnet. As the cycle rotates, it creates the energy that pulls the puzzle pieces together.

Rebuild America System™

Capital Growth Cycle
Stakeholders + Personal & Professional Capital Goals + Action

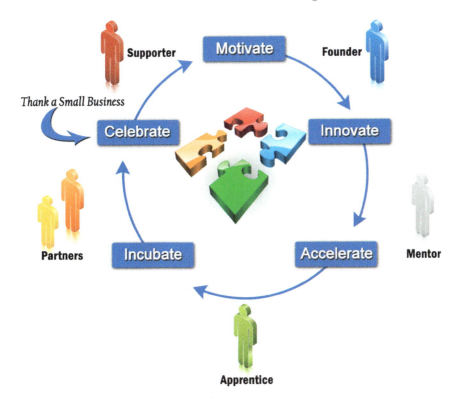

Chapter 22

Grassroots Capitalism. County-by-County.

No matter what stakeholder role you choose at a particular time—whether you're a Supporter, Founder, Mentor, Apprentice, or Partner—your growth will follow a similar action pattern. You hear an inspirational message from one of our events or from a local member who tells you what they discovered. Inspiration turns into motivation and you plug into your local market program.

Innovation, acceleration, incubation, and celebration mean different things to each stakeholder, but the process, pattern, and timeline are consistent. You set the agenda based on your role. You plug into the cycle at your pace, which connects you with other stakeholders on a parallel journey. Since you are in the Capital Growth Cycle with different stakeholder groups, the cross-pollination and brainstorming opportunities are significant.

For example, let's suppose a local county resident decides to found a new business.

Does she immediately know what programs, service organizations, mentors, and support systems are available to her? Not likely. Now let's imagine she attended a **Celebrate Small Business** Luncheon and heard about *The **MADE IN THE USA Project***™. If she first plugs into the local PATRIOT MISSION Chapter as an Apprentice, not only will she learn about Founder's resources, she will actually meet the people who are providing the support, meet mentors, and fellow apprentices.

She will observe Founders tell their stories and interface with Mentors and community Supporters who promote local vendors. She will be able to test her ideas by offering a "Patriot Pitch" in front of a live crowd who can give real, marketplace feedback before she ever risks a dime of capital. As a new Founder, by tapping into the local **Private Business Incubator**™, she is far more likely to succeed!

Time is our most precious commodity.

No matter what your role, every minute you save while pursuing your goals will help you be more productive. The previous example highlights one simple example of how the local chapter connects dots and saves time for a stakeholder. Whether you are an Apprentice looking for encouragement, a Founder in search of a Mentor to help take your business to the next level, or a Supporter trying to understand policy issues that impact local commerce, we all benefit from a trusted place to plug in and connect with like-minded people.

Obviously, it will take time before there are chapters operating in every county, independent city, and parish. That is one of the reasons we offer a subscription to our **Rebuild America Series**™ to connect all our members to what is happening around the country. You can access online resources, webcasts, teleconferences, and live events, just to name a few programs. Depending on your situation, you may want to learn about our partner programs to help open up your local community.

The following overviews will provide a good perspective on each of the three chapter programs. These descriptions will be general since our model is proprietary and continuously improving.

Local programs are adapted for each county chapter based on demographics and economic factors. We have training modules to help our members get a full understanding about the specific benefits, objectives, and functions of each program.

Celebrate Small Business™

Celebrating small business is how we begin to transition from inspiration to implementation. As people hear the "big picture" message about **Rebuilding America through the Power of Small Business**™, the next part of the process is to bring the idea into focus in the local marketplace. Think of the small companies you do business with in your area that do a great job. Other than your patronage, which is certainly important, how often do you think the community at large celebrates these entrepreneurs, their employees, and families?

The primary reason is because most consumers and patrons see a company, not the people who make the business work. The stories of key stakeholders are the connection that brings to life the heart and the passion behind the business. It is one thing to go to a nice local restaurant because you like the food. It's quite another when you enjoy the menu AND you know the back story of the owner. When you discover the personal journey and meaning behind the entrepreneur's passion to put an outstanding meal on your plate, the value of the relationship grows by an exponential factor.

Now imagine there is a concerted effort to collect and share the inspirational stories of the small business stakeholders in your community. This includes the entrepreneurs, supporters, mentors, and apprentices who are engaged in the capital growth cycle and power the local economy. Excitement spreads when entrepreneurial stories promoting your county, city, or parish as a great place to be in business are combined with supporting perspectives on living, working, and having fun in the area.

The effort to share these inspirational stories is a simple and effective way to **LEAD** Americans to Rediscover the "Shining City on a Hill." The reason is simple. The energy that lights up the city comes from thousands of free citizens who get up early, stay up late, and work incredibly hard to pursue their American dream.

In our fast-paced world, most people don't slow down long enough to tell stories or listen to them. When we do take the time, the value of the relationship with the other person goes up significantly. Making an effort to recognize, thank, and celebrate small businesses in a community, sends a strong message to owners and local residents. This is a team effort. Especially when an owner is facing tough times, this effort may make all the difference between staying open another day or not.

Leaders understand the value of people who make a community work and are willing to invest their time and resources to celebrate their success. Gathering the stories to **Celebrate Small Business**™ is how we begin to **BUILD** a Bold Leadership Team in every county, city, and parish. Leaders work with local stakeholders and our support team to organize, publish, and promote these powerful stories in multiple channels throughout the county, city, and parish. As the impact of the effort to **Celebrate Small Business**™ takes root, it will become a core element to cement grassroots capitalism in a local chapter.

The local leadership team will largely determine the pace, timing, and support to transition to *The **MADE IN THE USA Project***™, which drives the formal launch of the local chapter.

The **MADE IN THE USA Project**™

The goal of the project is to ignite the entrepreneurial spirit in a new generation by sharing stories of men and women who have experienced trials and triumphs in their pursuit of the American Dream! A key motivator in our entrepreneurial revolution is the frustration people experience with political decisions that have destroyed our manufacturing base and financial stability. By definition, small businesses are **MADE IN THE USA,** and we celebrate and promote them because they reinforce our capabilities to make products and services and create a strong economy.

America's recovery demands grassroots leadership. We don't have the luxury to continue business as usual. Entrepreneurs are leaders because they take responsibility for the outcome and they do not wait for someone else to do something. This project helps effectively and efficiently integrate leadership development into the business community on a broad scale.

"Leaders aren't born they are made. And they are made just like anything else, through hard work. And that's the price we'll have to pay to achieve that goal, or any goal."
—Vince Lombardi

When the local leadership team is satisfied the benchmarks have been reached, they coordinate with the national support group and initiate the project plan. *The **MADE IN THE USA Project**™* has three phases mapped out over approximately 18 months.

Phase 1: Publish the Success Stories of 12 Local Leaders in a book for each Chapter

Phase 2: Promote local Economic Development Resources, Organizations, and Mentors

Phase 3: Launch a 1 Year Leadership Development Program to Expand Local Growth

Once the decision is made to launch the chapter, the leadership team initiates the turnkey plan to kick-start *The **MADE IN**

THE USA Project™. This requires a strong core leadership team to step up and raise the seed capital to launch the project. This is easy to do using new crowd funding technologies and, most importantly, it makes sure everyone has some "skin in the game." It doesn't require a lot of money and it is simple, secure, and is managed with strong accountability. The key point is the community moves from conversation to grassroots action and each player makes a tangible, personal investment in the effort.

During the next six months, the pre-launch action plan builds momentum. The community hears the story and learns about a new book being published featuring local entrepreneurial leaders. Young people, job seekers, and veterans will be offered opportunities to learn from small business founders and experienced entrepreneurial mentors. Retired people, current employees, and public workers will be able to participate and show their support for local small businesses. Those who are in extremely financially challenging situations will be able to apply for Patriot Grants.

When all the preparations are complete, local leaders will host a community wide book launch event to celebrate entrepreneurship and spotlight local small business heroes whose stories are featured. The launch event will be fun, entertaining, and unique. Most importantly, it will not be a one-time event; rather, it is the beginning of a long-term plan to promote entrepreneurship and capitalism. The program will share local vision and explain how it integrates with other counties, cities, and parishes in their state, region, and nation.

Small business founders, apprentices, mentors, and capitalism enthusiasts will be invited to meet monthly for the next year to engage in a multi-faceted Leadership Development Program. The 12 monthly events develop core themes introduced at the launch and build the framework to support a unique, private business incubator in the community.

These fundamentals, reinforced over 18 months, create the

structure, understanding, and support to launch the next chapter based program to permanently drive grassroots capitalism deep and wide.

PATRIOT MISSION Private Business Incubator™

What is Business Incubation?

According to the National Business Incubation Association (NBIA), http://www.NBIA.org: "Business incubation is a business support process that accelerates the successful development of start-up and fledgling companies by providing entrepreneurs with an array of targeted resources and services. These services are usually developed or orchestrated by incubator management and offered both in the business incubator and through its network of contacts.

A business incubator's main goal is to produce successful firms that will leave the program financially viable and freestanding. These incubator graduates have the potential to create jobs, revitalize neighborhoods, commercialize new technologies, and strengthen local and national economies."

To be successful, the community has to be ready to support and participate in the incubation process. This is why investing the time in the community to **Celebrate Small Business**™ and doing hands-on work in *The MADE IN THE USA Project*™ are crucial. It is also why we include all community stakeholders, because we believe everyone who understands the Power of Small Business can contribute to the process.

One of my early motivations for creating this model was thinking about the reason so many small businesses fail. There are a myriad of reasons, but at the heart of the matter is that people who start businesses don't usually go through a preparation process.

Michael Gerber says the skilled technician who is competent at delivering a product or service wakes up one day and has an entrepreneurial seizure. He decides to fire his boss, go into business, and suddenly finds himself working for a lunatic. What if this guy could be an apprentice before he has a seizure?

Here's another stimulating question. How much intellectual property goes to the grave every year because there is no strategy to capture lessons learned and infuse them into the next generation?

According to a study conducted by the University of Michigan and NBIA, entitled Business Incubation Works, **87% of business incubation graduates stay in business**. NBIA estimates there are approximately 1200 incubators in the USA and 7000 total around the world. In the next seven years, we intend to add at least 3141 creative new **Private Business Incubators**™ to the total.

According to NBIA, less than 10% of incubators are owned by for-profit companies. Most are run by government, local economic development agencies, or educational institutions, not by experienced entrepreneurs. Our for-profit incubators will be run by qualified entrepreneurs who have faced the trials and triumphs of business. We focus on profitable mentoring and leadership development through a number of proprietary systems. We will revolutionize American and global entrepreneurship.

Most incubators have historically focused on a very small number of start-up participants. In recent years, there has been a shift to bring more than shared office space and training to fledgling companies. "*Business Accelerators*" have added vital elements of capital acquisition and angel investing primarily to market specific start-ups, like bio-tech or software companies.

If you recall, the second phase of *The **MADE IN THE USA Project**™* brings together organizations in the community that support small business. One of the primary reasons for this is to plant the seeds to build a local incubator. In your county or within a drive to a neighboring county, you may find an existing business incubator hidden in plain sight.

You might be surprised what your local state or community college has in place. Oftentimes, there are tremendous resources available, but seizing entrepreneurs running on adrenaline have no idea they exist.

The PATRIOT MISSION model is about connecting the dots in a county, not recreating the wheel. The original premise of our work is the resources already exist in most places but up until now, there has been no effective way to pull together the diverse elements of the community to support small business. America is motivated to look at things differently because of the perilous times in which we live. Resources are tight. We need to use everything we have more effectively.

Our chapter based network of **Private Business Incubators**™ will be an essential tool to **Rebuild America through the Power of Small Business**™.

Who runs the chapter and manages implementation?

The Bold Leadership Team is comprised of PATRIOT MISSION Partners and local stakeholders. These are the people who have decided to invest time, energy, and resources in these programs. The motivations for each are different.

For example, the Partners are focused on the business opportunity represented by profitably operating a chapter and serving its members. The Supporter is often motivated by investing in the next generation and serving the community. Mentors are typically those entrepreneurs with decades of intellectual property in their heads who want to teach others what they know.

There will be people who play a key role at different times in the chapter development. It is important to give this process the time to become integrated into the community. That's why it's called grassroots capitalism. To be successful over the long term, those in the county, city, or parish must be the driving force to make it successful. The combination of a Bold Leadership Team, a supportive PATRIOT MISSION national organization and fellow chapter organizations creates a firm foundation for success.

How long will it take to implement grassroots capitalism in local chapters?

These three programs will be integrated in a community over a period of months and years. In case you are getting ready to yell and tell me we don't have years to get the country rebuilt, I respectfully ask you to dial the volume down. I get the point, understand it, and agree with you.

There are certain actions that require afterburner right now and we'll discuss those near the end of the book. We will dump raw fuel in the afterburners for massive short-term acceleration. At the same time, we are putting in place long-term solutions to empower grassroots capitalism to grow and thrive in the future. We need both.

The first two strategies of the **Rebuild America System**™ are designed to create a lot of energy quickly. When you simultaneously **Inspire A Nation** and **Implement Grassroots Chapters,** you can get local operations airborne and keep them flying for the long haul. These three programs are built to accomplish self-sustained short, medium, and long-term goals.

1. **Celebrate Small Business**™

2. ***The MADE IN THE USA Project***™

3. **PATRIOT MISSION Private Business Incubator**™

Implementing grassroots capitalism is analogous to the planning, design, horsepower, and professionalism required to get an airplane off the runway, complete the mission, and land safely. It doesn't matter whether the mission is transporting passengers or air-to-air combat, there are basic rules of engineering, flight planning, ground operations, propulsion, aerodynamics, fuel management, target acquisition, mutual support, and safety which must be adhered to or you will crash and burn.

The way I see it, we are on a mission for all the marbles. There are a lot of people in panic mode precisely because they do not know what to do. These are also people who are willing to be led if the people who are leading have a real plan. It's also why we need a Bold Leadership Team in each county. Bold leaders do not live in fear. Bold leaders have the guts to look terrified people in the eyes and tell them there is a plan. We have it. Come join us.

America is in the shape it's in because many people have abdicated their responsibility to lead. It was easier to go along and get along. That time, my friends, is over. We are watching the daily destruction of our magnificent, constitutionally based republic, and if we don't lead, who will?

In 1961, President John F. Kennedy told America we would land a man on the moon and return him safely to Earth before the decade was out. At the time he spoke, the technology did not exist to complete the mission. America looked to the heavens and got focused on solving the problems so Neil Armstrong and his crew could land on the moon on July 20, 1969, and splash down safely in the Pacific Ocean on July 24, 1969.

I know we are facing enormous challenges, but I also know with God's leading and our principle based focus, we can succeed at this mission and save our republic. Right now, you can be sure the world is watching. People around the globe are wondering if America is swirling in the bowl of human history like so many great civilizations before us.

Millions of people are looking at you and me for leadership. They are peering through the fence at men and women who are American entrepreneurs. They are watching how we handle both our business and our freedom. What we do individually and collectively will impact global entrepreneurship, the world's economy, and so much more. With all our troubles in America, why should we care about our influence on global entrepreneurs? Let's talk about that.

Chapter 23

Strategy #3—Influence Global Entrepreneurship

It may seem like an oxymoron when I suggest that in order to complete our mission to **Rebuild America through the Power of Small Business**™, we must also influence global entrepreneurship. If we are so concerned with what's happening within our borders and we are already limited on time and resources, then why look outside the fence? That's a fair question.

I acknowledge we have our hands full here at home inspiring a nation and implementing grassroots capitalism. The reality is American business people already influence global entrepreneurship. The question is which business people and what type of influence is being foisted on our international friends. The obvious answer is big business has the most influence on the global spectrum. Certainly in terms of money and political influence that is true. However, I suggest the small business community can become a much bigger influence on the global stage and for more people.

Just like earlier discussions we've had about the numbers of U.S. small businesses, when you influence 10% of 30 million entrepreneurs, you can have an impact. The same is true worldwide. With the rapid explosion of social media and smart phones around the globe, our work can have a massive impact and reach millions of people in short order.

Promote Capitalism & Freedom

The primary reason we have to work so hard now is because complacency has eaten our lunch for decades. We've allowed America to devolve into the current conditions. Given the option to let the country burn to the ground or rebuild, we choose to go to work. What do you think will happen as entrepreneurs and would-be capitalists watch us Rebuild America? Do think it will inspire them? Certainly it will.

Global entrepreneurship covers an enormous spectrum from First-World industrialized nations to emerging countries and the impoverished Third World. Each has its own set of circumstances, challenges, and relationship with the United States. For the sake of brevity, we are going to focus on what they all have in common.

Every global nation, whether economically strong or destitute, is comprised of people. People who want to take care of themselves and their families.

Freedom is a fundamental human right. When we celebrate our unalienable, God-given right to use our freedom productively, we encourage others who long to be free. They may live in countries that allow some cottage industry, but make it difficult. Perhaps they have to go through miles of red tape before they can open an enterprise. In some places, they get a fun-loving partner called the government, whether they want a partner or not. In the poorest countries, just the opportunity to make the equivalent of a dollar or two a week can determine if a family eats or has clean water.

Freedom is the fuel that powers the streetlamps of the "Shining City on a Hill." This light gives people hope that maybe someday they can have freedom, too. That is why those who have escaped oppression and get to America are so disgusted with what we have allowed to happen to our country. Most Americans have no idea how truly blessed we are.

This conversation comes down to a simple point illustrated by two rhetorical questions.

Is America better off when people around the world are pursuing freedom and capitalism?

Or conversely, are we in a stronger position when people succumb to tyrannical governments, oppressive regimes, or socialist utopians?

These despotic forms of government have a much easier time controlling their people when their subjects are not inspired to peacefully resist and pursue their skills, talents, and strengths through grassroots capitalism. With every step we take to Rebuild America, we turn up the intensity of the streetlights and increase the candlepower so our cities can be seen from farther and farther away.

Expand Markets & Sales

In addition to setting a good example for others around the world and igniting a spark of capitalism, what practical steps can we take to build relationships with global entrepreneurs?

As we Rebuild America, we should build connections with kindred spirits in other countries. This does not necessarily mean we need to transact business right away, but I do believe expanding our networks with like-minded entrepreneurs around the world is productive. Many of my closest business friends and colleagues are our northern neighbors in Canada. Learning other cultures, studying their history and business climates is productive because it gives us perspective.

For illustration purposes, let's discuss two simple global opportunities that can enhance our local, regional, or national businesses here in the USA. Since the Internet is the most powerful business tool ever created, we can use it to find just about anything we want with the click of a mouse.

Do you provide a product or service that can be delivered outside your local market?

How can you use the Internet to find companies, vendors, suppliers, resellers, or other joint venture partners who will buy or resell your American made product or service in key markets around the world?

Obviously, there are many variables that will dictate how you handle this question; but the point of the exercise is to think beyond your local town. For some businesses, local market is nearly all their business, but in almost every case I've seen, even with a physical product or service that is delivered locally, there are creative deliverables that can be sold through the Internet. When you add profitable revenue streams, you strengthen your local business.

Upgrade Your Products & Services

The second opportunity is to find other companies you can hire to upgrade your product or service offering for your local, national, and international markets. Most entrepreneurs get myopic when it comes to their "*baby.*" Sometimes, doing it all yourself is the kiss of death if it means you can't compete. We need to stay true to our principles, keep focused on our strengths, and remain profitable.

Brainstorming these types of ideas with your local team is a great way to expand your thinking. You will be surprised by the amount of experience others in your area have when it comes to doing business outside your market. Most importantly, you get stronger and more effective when you think beyond your office walls. The beauty of brainstorming is you can quickly discern if an idea has merit or is probably one destined for the recycle bin. In either case, you get stronger.

Stronger American entrepreneurs are good. Enhanced bottom lines with multiple revenue streams are very good. At the end of the day, building strong small businesses is the best hedge we have against tyranny. Doing the work that is in our personal best interest is inspiring to people in our local community. As a part of a growing base of American entrepreneurs, you become an inspiration to entrepreneurs living everywhere between the four corners of the Earth.

Over the coming years, PATRIOT MISSION International will work with global partners to offer our programs to freedom-loving entrepreneurs around the globe. Make no mistake about it. Your success story will not only inspire your fellow Americans but will influence entrepreneurs around the world. There will come a day when you will have the opportunity to tell your story on a global stage. Most importantly, the compounded impact of stories from our American Entrepreneurial Revolution will do more for freedom around the world than any armed conflict ever could.

PART IV

HOW CAN I WIN BY HELPING REBUILD AMERICA?

"Dream boldly and savor the consequences."

– Robert Olds –

Chapter 24

2020 Storyline & Beyond

Have you ever wondered why you were chosen to live on Earth at this moment in time?

This is an amazing time to be alive. We are living in the midst of the most transformational time in human history and we get to decide which way the story ends; well, at least the part of the story that depends on what we do. From the scriptures I read, God has made it crystal clear how His story ends. All we have to decide is what we believe to be our calling, who we serve, and whether we are willing to go to work. Simple enough, I guess.

The two storylines for 2020 America are pretty simple.

Option A: **America Destroyed**
Option B: **America Rebuilt**

It's not hard to get to Option A. All you have to do is take this book and use it for kindling or throw it in the recycle bin. Ignore America's foundational history and everything in this story. Continue forth building the unachievable utopian state. Give your family a kiss good-bye and tell them it was too much trouble to fight for them. Even if you have the mindset to believe a socialist economy can work (*despite all the reams of evidence to the contrary*), you are sentencing your family to indentured servitude and state-sponsored oppression.

That was easy. Pour yourself a cocktail, tell yourself you really mean well, do absolutely nothing to rebuild the nation, and you can guarantee Option A is the winner.

Well, there is one problem with the aforementioned guarantee. I should have said, Option A is the winner **IF** you can convince every one of the **BOLD** leaders who is engaged in this Entrepreneurial Revolution to Rebuild America through the Power of Small Business, to lay down and quit.

Something about another world freezing over comes to mind. More to the point, to quote a few close relatives when queried on submitting to what amounts to a hostile takeover of America: *"Absolutely not. We have not fought for our country to just roll over and let it be destroyed!"*

Option B requires a decision to stand up and fight for what we believe. It is easy to say we want to **Rebuild America through the Power of Small Business**™. It has a nice ring to it. To actually do the work and be successful in the face of Goliath, we need to follow a master blueprint, build a world-class team, and execute flawlessly. And just to be clear, our back is against the wall.

We don't have any more time for false starts or do-overs.

We need a big team with strong leaders cascading and growing throughout the organization. We need leaders and team members who are willing to do their part for the long haul. And make no mistake, the question of allegiance will come up over and over. This is the road less traveled. It's the hard choice, but it's the honorable choice. Just like rebuilding lower Manhattan after 9/11, it's the only choice for Americans. It's the choice that guarantees you can hold your head up high when your kids and grandkids ask what part you played in Rebuilding America.

What will the long, strange trip look like?

You and I both know it's easy to map out a plan, build a few prototypes, and project a nice simple model across the country from sea to shining sea. The hard part is following through when you know going in there are many cowardly adversaries lurking in the shadows. As Major Bach said so eloquently, you know as a leader you are going to work harder than anyone else. You will give of yourself in ways you can't imagine. Why? Because it's the right thing to do. While we can't know exactly what will happen, we do know we are prepared to go to work.

This reminds me of a very hot, muggy Virginia day in August 1990.

One day we are jawing about going to the Officer's Club on Friday night and taking a weekend trip to Virginia Beach. The next day we are skipping happy hour and planning a trip to a completely different sandbox.

We had no idea what was coming. We were told to pack our bags and get ready for a 14-hour, non-stop flight in a single seat, fully armed F-15 with a one-way flight plan to a war zone. No idea how long we'll be gone, whether everyone will come back, what the casualties will be... nothing but unknowns, except two. We were trained to fight and we knew why we were going. We believed in the oath we took to Protect and Defend the Constitution of the United States against all enemies, foreign and domestic. Murdering thugs invaded Kuwait and we stood against them.

As I alluded to in my January 16, 2011 flashback, at this moment in history, we are here to stand against soft tyranny. We are facing those who believe it is permissible to operate outside the confines of the Constitution. We beg to differ. We are not subjects, we are citizens. We may be in the minority… for the moment, but we will proceed with vigor because we have pledged our lives, our fortunes, and our sacred honor.

The choice is ours. We fight for freedom using the local marketplace as our battlefield or we settle for the fundamental transformation of America away from our founding principles. If we choose Liberty, we must take action. As for me and my house, we will serve the Lord and his gift to the world: the United States of America.

What will *America Rebuilt* look like in 2020?

In Chapter 2, I said we get to determine the action sequence that will be written. While we cannot specifically control outcome, we can, by our very intention, set the course to complete our mission to **Rebuild America through the Power of Small Business**™.

While the know-it-all pundits will enjoy mocking me for the idiocy of trying to rally 30M people behind this idea, we will be about our business deep in the grassroots of America. Fortunately, most of the grassroots is in "flyover" country, which means the elites pay very little attention to it.

Mission Accomplished: Here's a snapshot of the successful Dream, Vision, Purpose, and Mission in terms of the **3 I's**: inspire, implement, and influence.

1. When we **LEAD** Americans to Rediscover the "Shining City on a Hill," then **inspired** Americans will embrace our **7 Founding LIBERTY Principles**, reject political correctness, and accurately teach the next generation our unique national story.

2. When we **BUILD** Bold Leadership Teams in every county, independent city, and parish, thenGrassroots

Capitalism will be flourishing with at least 3141 chapters **implemented** with operational Private Business Incubators and over 30,000,000 members.

3. When we **GROW** our Capital, Political Influence, and Liberty, then American entrepreneurs will **influence** policy and collaborate with global leaders because we will have helped reestablish a vibrant U.S. economy driven by sound fiscal policy and core freedom values.

Now, all we have to do is make a decision on what to do personally. Cheerleading is fine, but we prefer players on the field. Before we finish up and review the options, I'd like to share a story that always motivates me. I'm not a biblical scholar by any means, but if you want a phenomenal lesson in leadership, pull out the Old Testament and read the book of Nehemiah.

This is a guy who was the cupbearer to the King, deep inside the inner circle. Then he gets word that his hometown, the city of Jerusalem, has been destroyed. The big walls were knocked down, the city gates burned and the people pummeled. Nehemiah boldly approached the King and asked for a leave of absence, loads of supplies, and safe passage. The King could have had Nehemiah executed for having a despondent spirit in the inner sanctum, but he was inspired and granted the request.

Nehemiah was attacked from many directions, physically, emotionally, and politically. He went deep into the grassroots and got local families and shopkeepers to work together and focus on the enormous project of Rebuilding Jerusalem. Most thought it impossible, but since Nehemiah was clearly inspired (by God himself), the people went along with it. Each day they got stronger and more productive. They eventually bought into the idea the wall could actually be rebuilt.

Even facing possible attacks, the men worked in shifts, held swords with their tools, checked each others' six and most importantly, never quit. They watched the politicians try to bribe and threaten Nehemiah, who skillfully rebuked their character assassination and legal maneuvers.

The wall was rebuilt, charred gates replaced, and a nation inspired in **52 DAYS**! ***Impossible?***

I refer you to another scripture that has seen me through many challenging times: Mathew 19:26 where Jesus says: "With man this is impossible, but with God all things are possible."

I believe this Word is as true today as the moment it was written. If Jerusalem can be rebuilt by a team of committed, God-fearing families, then I believe America can be, too. This will confound the wise and cause millions of people to discover why America's founding on Judeo-Christian heritage is vital. This is the 2020 storyline I'm sticking with: impossible for man—easy for God.

Now there is only one question left. What are you going to do?

Chapter 25

"Fight's On"

"Fight's On" is a term we use in the flying business when our operational checks are complete and we are ready to engage our adversary. The last cockpit switch to move is the MASTER ARM toggle. The moment you reach up and arm that switch, the little red button under your thumb is all that stands between you and sending your adversary to meet his maker.

So figuratively speaking, it's time to decide if you are ready to engage your personal MASTER ARM switch and head into the fight... or not. It's a simple question.

Are you in or are you out?

I'm not going to bog down the end of our time together with a sophisticated pitch to encourage you to do one thing or another. Believe me, if I have to talk you into being here, then I have to talk you into staying here. I'll pass on that. There will be time later to decide which stakeholder role suits you best, but by now you should have an idea of how **YOU WIN** by helping us.

As you contemplate the proposal on the table, think deeply about the impact your decision will have on your family for generations to come. What could your legacy be for our nation? Take some time and think it through and then decide if you are for us or against us.

We have purposely built our case to be black or white. There is no grey area. America destroyed or America Rebuilt? Yes or No? There are no wrong answers. After you read this final, historical perspective, I'll give you a website address where you can take 10 seconds, make your decision known, and get your personal blueprint.

Before you do, I want you to read the words of a man who faced similar circumstances in 1775.

Obviously, Patrick Henry is referring to armed conflict and we are not, but I believe you'll find many of his thoughts and frustrations eerily similar to ours. Most people who have a working knowledge of history can probably quote the entire last line of this speech, but his words from beginning to end are powerful. This is yet another example of why we must study our history and pass it on to the next generation.

So take your time, read it slowly and then make your decision.

LIBERTY OR DEATH[3]
March 23, 1775

"NO man thinks more highly than I do of the patriotism, as well as abilities, of the very worthy gentlemen who have just addressed the House. But different men often see the same subject in different lights; and, therefore, I hope that it will not be thought disrespectful to those gentlemen, if entertaining, as I do, opinions of a character very opposite to theirs, I shall speak forth my sentiments freely, and without reserve. This is no time for ceremony. The question before the House is one of awful moment to this country. For my own part, I consider it as nothing less than a question of freedom or slavery. And in proportion to the magnitude of the subject, ought to be the freedom of the debate. It is only in this way that we can hope to arrive at truth and fulfill the great responsibility which we hold to God and our country. Should I keep back my opinions at such a time, through fear of giving offense, I should consider myself as guilty of treason towards my country and of an act of disloyalty towards the majesty of Heaven which I revere above all earthly kings.

Mr. President it is natural to man to indulge in the illusions of hope. We are apt to shut our eyes against a painful truth—and listen to the song of the siren till she transforms us into beasts. Is this the part of wise men engaged in a great and arduous struggle for liberty? Are we disposed to be of the number of those who, having eyes, see not, and having ears, hear not, the things which so nearly concern their temporal salvation? For my part, whatever anguish of spirit it may cost, I am willing to know the whole truth; to know the worst and to provide for it.

I have but one lamp by which my feet are guided; and that is the lamp of experience. I know of no way of judging of the future but by the past. And judging by the past, I wish to know what there has been in the conduct of the British ministry for the last ten years to justify those hopes with which gentlemen have been pleased to solace themselves and the house? Is it that insidious smile with which our petition has been lately received? Trust it not, sir; it will prove a snare to your feet. Suffer not yourselves to be betrayed with a kiss. Ask yourselves how this gracious reception of our petition comports with these warlike preparations which cover our waters and darken our land. Are fleets and armies necessary to a work of love and reconciliation? Have we shown ourselves so unwilling to be reconciled that force must be called in to win back our love? Let us not deceive ourselves, sir. These are the implements of war and subjugation—the last arguments to which kings resort.

I ask gentlemen, sir, what means this martial array if its purpose be not to force us to submission? Can gentlemen assign any other possible motives for it? Has Great Britain any enemy, in this quarter of the world to call for all this accumulation of navies and armies? No, sir, she has none. They are meant for us: they can be meant for no other. They are sent over to bind and rivet upon us those chains which the British ministry have been so long forging.

And what have we to oppose to them? Shall we try argument? Sir, we have been trying that for the last ten years. Have we anything new to offer on the subject? Nothing. We have held the subject up in every light of which it is capable; but it has been all in vain. Shall we resort to entreaty and humble supplication? What terms shall we find which have not been already exhausted?

Let us not, I beseech you, sir, deceive ourselves longer. Sir, we have done everything that could be done to avert the storm which is now coming on. We have petitioned—we have remonstrated—we have supplicated—we have prostrated ourselves before the throne, and have implored its interposition to arrest the tyrannical hands of the ministry and Parliament. Our petitions have been slighted; our remonstrances have produced additional violence and insult; our supplications have been disregarded; and we have been spurned, with contempt, from the foot of the throne.

In vain, after these things, may we indulge the fond hope of peace and reconciliation. There is no longer any room for hope. If we wish to be free—if we mean to preserve inviolate those inestimable privileges for which we have been so long contending—if we mean not basely to abandon the noble struggle in which we have been so long engaged, and which we have pledged ourselves never to abandon until the glorious object of our contest shall be obtained—we must fight! I repeat it, sir, we must fight! An appeal to arms and to the God of Hosts is all that is left us!

They tell us, sir, that we are weak—unable to cope with so formidable an adversary. But when shall we be stronger? Will it be the next week, or the next year? Will it be when we are totally disarmed, and when a British guard shall be stationed in every house? Shall we gather strength by irresolution and inaction? Shall we acquire the means of effectual resistance by lying supinely on our backs, and hugging the delusive phantom of Hope, until our enemies shall have bound us hand and foot?

Sir, we are not weak, if we make a proper use of the means which the God of nature hath placed in our power. Three millions of people, armed in the holy cause of liberty, and in such a country as that which we possess, are invincible by any force which our enemy can send against us.

Besides, sir, we shall not fight our battles alone. There is a just God who presides over the destinies of nations, and who will raise up friends to fight our battles for us. The battle, sir, is not to the strong alone; it is to the vigilant, the active, the brave. Besides, sir, we have no election. If we were base enough to desire it, it is now too late to retire from the contest. There is no retreat, but in submission and slavery! Our chains are forged, their clanking may be heard on the plains of Boston! The war is inevitable—and let it come! I repeat it, sir, let it come!

It is in vain, sir, to extenuate the matter. Gentlemen may cry, peace, peace—but there is no peace. The war is actually begun. The next gale that sweeps from the north will bring to our ears the clash of resounding arms! Our brethren are already in the field! Why stand we here idle? What is it that gentlemen wish? What would they have? Is life so dear, or peace so sweet, as to be purchased at the price of chains and slavery? Forbid it, Almighty God! I know not what course others may take; but as for me, give me liberty, or give me death!"

Enough said.

Now it's time for action. You can choose to be a Supporter, Founder, Mentor, or Apprentice. You can also inquire about becoming a PATRIOT MISSION Partner and helping us engage and grow this massive vision in the marketplace.

We are building a big team. We need leaders and a lot of players to help America win. Together, we will develop a strong, powerful, and vibrant Patriot Community to support every American who wants to dream again. Together, alongside millions of other patriots who are working diligently in their areas of expertise, we will restore the fading American Dream into the vibrant promise that our ancestors fought to pass on to our generation.

Register at http://www.PatriotProfile.com and we'll send you a personalized blueprint to help you get started in your position of strength as we lead an American Entrepreneurial Revolution.

It will be great to have you on our team. Our country needs you... now!

Fight's On.

Get your FREE Personal Blueprint to Rebuild America through the Power of Small Business™

Call Toll Free: 855.TO.REBUILD
(855.867.3284) or Visit
http://www.PatriotProfile.com

Receive a Bonus Subscription to the "Rebuild America Series™" when you claim your personal blueprint!

CLIENT: *Your Name*
PROJECT: *Rebuild America*

REFERENCES

1. President Reagan's Farewell Address to the Nation, January 11, 198
   http://www.reaganfoundation.org/
   http://www.reagan.utexas.edu/archives/speeches/1989/011189i.htm

2. Major C.A. Bach, Farewell Instructions to the Graduating Student Officers of the Second Training Camp at Fort Sheridan, Wyoming, in 1917.
   http://www.au.af.mil/au/awc/awcgate/au-24/bach.pdf

3. Patrick Henry, "Liberty or Death"
   http://www.patrickhenrycenter.com/Speeches.aspx#LIBERTY

Dictionary Bibliography

1. "revolution." Collins English Dictionary—Complete & Unabridged 10th Edition. HarperCollins Publishers. 13 Aug. 2013. <Dictionary.com http://dictionary.reference.com/browse/revolution>.

2. "patriot." Dictionary.com Unabridged. Random House, Inc. 13 Aug. 2013. <Dictionary.com http://dictionary.reference.com/browse/patriot>.

3. "liberty." Dictionary.com Unabridged. Random House, Inc. 13 Aug. 2013. <Dictionary.com http://dictionary.reference.com/browse/liberty>.

4. "entrepreneur." Dictionary.com Unabridged. Random House, Inc. 13 Aug. 2013. <Dictionary.com http://dictionary.reference.com/browse/entrepreneur>.

5. "capitalism." Dictionary.com Unabridged. Random House, Inc. 13 Aug. 2013. <Dictionary.com http://dictionary.reference.com/browse/capitalism>.

6. "free enterprise." Dictionary.com Unabridged. Random House, Inc. 13 Aug. 2013. <Dictionary.com http://dictionary.reference.com/browse/free enterprise>.

7. "American dream." Dictionary.com Unabridged. Random House, Inc. 13 Aug. 2013. <Dictionary.com http://dictionary.reference.com/browse/american dream>.

8. "leader." Author personal definition

9. "American freedom." Author personal definition

10. "bold." Dictionary.com Unabridged. Random House, Inc. 13 Aug. 2013. <Dictionary.com http://dictionary.reference.com/browse/bold>.

11. "capital." Dictionary.com Unabridged. Random House, Inc. 13 Aug. 2013. <Dictionary.com http://dictionary.reference.com/browse/capital>.

12. "success." Dictionary.com Unabridged. Random House, Inc. 13 Aug. 2013. <Dictionary.com http://dictionary.reference.com/browse/success>.

13. "teamwork." Dictionary.com Unabridged. Random House, Inc. 13 Aug. 2013. <Dictionary.com http://dictionary.reference.com/browse/teamwork>.

14. "liberty." Dictionary.com Unabridged. Random House, Inc. 13 Aug. 2013. <Dictionary.com http://dictionary.reference.com/browse/liberty>.

15. "tyranny." Dictionary.com Unabridged. Random House, Inc. 13 Aug. 2013. <Dictionary.com http://dictionary.reference.com/browse/tyranny>.

16. "stakeholder." Dictionary.com Unabridged. Random House, Inc. 13 Aug. 2013. <Dictionary.com http://dictionary.reference.com/browse/stakeholder>.

NOTES:

NOTES:

CPSIA information can be obtained at www.ICGtesting.com
Printed in the USA
LVOW02*0749060614

388889LV00001B/1/P